Nature Sparks

Also by Aerial Cross

Ants in Their Pants: Teaching Children Who Must Move to Learn
Come and Play: Sensory-Integration Strategies for Children with Play Challenges

Nature Sparks

Connecting

CHILDREN'S LEARNING

to the

NATURAL

WORLD

Aerial Cross

Redleaf Press®
www.redleafpress.org
800-423-8309

Published by Redleaf Press
10 Yorkton Court
St. Paul, MN 55117
www.redleafpress.org

First edition 2012
Cover design by Jim Handrigan
Cover photograph © Jacqueline Southby/Veer
Interior design by Jim Handrigan
Interior typeset in Janson and Trade Gothic
Illustrations by Claire Schipke
Printed in the United States of America
18 17 16 15 14 13 12 11   1 2 3 4 5 6 7 8

This book contains the names of products and websites and the companies that produce them. Neither the author nor Redleaf Press endorses or sells any of the products mentioned and is not affiliated with any of the businesses that produce them. Redleaf Press is not responsible for any dissatisfaction you may experience with any of the products or businesses referred to herein. All recommended websites and online games, supplies, utensils, and activities should be used at the discretion of the reader.

Library of Congress Cataloging-in-Publication Data
Cross, Aerial.
  Nature sparks : connecting children's learning to the natural world / Aerial Cross. — 1st ed.
    p. cm.
  Includes bibliographical references.
  ISBN 978-1-60554-041-2 (alk. paper)
  1. Nature study—United States. 2. Nature study—Activity programs.   I. Title.
LB1585.3.C75 2011
372.35'7—dc22
                                                        2011014189

Printed on FSC®-certified paper

To my sister, Sarah—
what mattered to you still matters to me.

Contents

Acknowledgments

PJ, Farrah, and Bella—you continue to amaze me!

My students—you teach me!

Eileen and Shawn—you show me the power of girlfriends!

Introduction

The idea for this book began gnawing at me after spending time with a beautiful American Indian girl named Luca. Luca and I were destined to meet after I received a phone call from an educator I had worked with for several years, who also happened to be a close friend. Luca was experiencing difficulties in school, and her teacher had concerns of a possible speech delay and learning disability. I agreed to visit the girl at home to give a third opinion.

As I ventured to Luca's home, which was on the New Mexico Indian Reservation, the barren land seemed endless. I eventually pulled up to the house and noticed the small girl standing next to an old Ford pickup hood.

As I got out of my car, I greeted her parents, then heard, "*Luca, ko' biyi'déé' hanilyeed!*" (translation: "Luca, move out of the hot pit!"). As Luca darted from underneath the Ford hood, I realized it covered a large hole in the ground. I walked up to her. She was engrossed in dirt, ash, and water play—strategically scooping the mixture to avoid getting any on her moccasins or on the half-nibbled corncob she clutched.

"You know sheeps are really dumbed?" she questioned me instantly.

"They aren't too smart," I chuckled, bending down in the dirt toward her and admiring the messy smudges on her tiny face.

"Sheeps always wanders off. Me's and my daddy has to always goes finds them," she stated before scurrying off behind her house. I followed her and discovered a natural and magical playground. Together, Luca and I engaged in connected, nature-driven play for several hours. We took turns hurling dried corncobs into a compost bin. Luca explained how her daddy kept the bin from getting "smellies." Luca pointed out her kitties' and puppies' paw tracks, detailing how they were different from her "sheeps'." We picked corn from the family's massive garden and placed several ears in the fire pit. She shared ways to use the corn silk. We climbed and jumped off the huge hay bales that surrounded the sheep corral. We rolled tumbleweeds with branches. Luca and I threw small dirt clods and rocks onto the sheet-metal roof that covered the family's recycling bins. Luca informed me of the special sounds: "The rocks *ping*, and the dirt clods *plop*." In an old cast-iron skillet, we mixed up a hearty batch of muddy "mutton stew" and "fry bread" from dirt, leaves, and water.

Luca's parents spoke the Navajo language and encouraged her to become fluent in it. Her family was immersed in their home language, which was different from what was taught at school. Luca possessed a strong drive to understand and learn words in English and continually asked, "How does you says this?" I noted her frustration when unable to express her thoughts. She'd clench and shake her little hands, then proceed to aggressively fiddle with her moccasins while mumbling under her breath. Her disposition turned aggressive until she found her words.

While Luca's English-language communication skills were weak, she never stopped talking or asking questions. The context of her conversation was meaningful. Further, many of her basic learning skills—observation and classification, predicting, experimenting, and interpreting—were strong. As we played together, Luca naturally demonstrated to me that she could solve problems independently and quickly. She created hearty and stimulating play that was driven entirely by her natural environment.

After the visit, I made several suggestions to both her teacher and family:

- Luca was in love with nature and animals. Everything about the outdoors intrigued her. It was no surprise to me when her parents stated they had to reluctantly drag her in most nights for dinner, covered in dirt. I suggested they connect the child to the outdoors for home chores and after-school activities as much as possible. Children learn best in open-ended exploration when connections are made.

- Luca combined English and her native tongue to express her feelings and thoughts. I asked that they determine what Luca might be attempting to communicate by looking closely at her body language, especially prior to aggressive actions. Ask her to repeat her requests using direct eye contact, while looking closely for signs of understanding in her hand and face gestures.

- I emphasized it was in Luca's best interest that her family and teacher work as a team to improve her language skills, yet continue to nurture her native tongue. Her parents valued literacy and wanted Luca to be fluently bilingual. Although culturally and linguistically diverse, they saw bilingualism for what it was—a powerful future tool for Luca. I stressed how Luca's motivation to acquire a new language would strengthen if it were connected to her passion—nature! In the classroom I encouraged her teacher to let Luca tell stories of her nature-play experiences to the class using English and her native tongue because it would assist her language skills—and Luca's bilingualism was also a gift to her classmates. I recommended that classroom and home items be labeled with both English and Navajo words alongside nature-oriented pictures to spark Luca's interest. Labels should have large, dark block letters on light backgrounds (black on white) (Watson and McCathren 2009).

pencil
bee 'ak'e'elchíhí

flower
ch'illátah hózhóón

For better understanding of what was implemented for Luca, look at the sample illustration on the right.

Luca is currently performing well in school. My suspicions were confirmed—a developmental delay did not exist. She is in a regular classroom keeping her teacher on her toes. Fortunately, her parents were receptive to my suggestions. Luca's vocabulary has exploded; she is nearly fluent in both English and Navajo.

Why I Wrote This Book

Keeping children connected to the natural world has always been an important aspect of early childhood growth and development. Unfortunately, children today are spending less and less time in nature (Rosenow 2008). This is unfortunate, because research shows that children benefit profoundly from regular interactions with nature. Studies demonstrate that contact with nature is as vital to children as proper sleep and nutrition. Strong positive correlations exist between outdoor play spaces and the relief of many behavioral and emotional disorders such as attention deficit hyperactivity disorder (ADHD) (Rosenow 2008). Educators face a challenge: children are becoming increasingly disconnected to the natural world, and this disconnection adversely affects their physical, emotional, and psychological health. It is disheartening.

I wrote this book to make educators aware of nature's monumental power on children's growth and development in a simple and straightforward way. Providing early experiences in the outdoors is the most important way educators can nurture concern for the environment in children (Wilson 1997). Outdoor experiences also help them develop personal health. Every parent and educator should make a goal of sharing and nurturing nature's miracles with children, especially in this increasingly materialistic and technology-driven world. The benefits nature brings to children's lives are enormous:

- Children regularly exposed to natural elements—such as fresh air, sunshine, and open meadows—feel better about themselves and are better able to cope with stress, anxiety, and depression. Research suggests that "the greater the amount of nature exposure, the greater the benefits" (Keeler 2008, 294).

- Children with attention deficit disorder (ADD) experience fewer symptoms of ADD while in nature. Again, "the greener the setting, the more the relief" (Keeler 2008, 294). Natural green environments emit a sense of peace and tranquility. While outdoors, children are more likely to observe small details and produce focused thoughts and creative ideas.

- Children who regularly play outdoors develop stronger gross-motor skills and show signs of better overall health than children who do not (Keeler 2008). To learn more about how naturalized outdoor environments, play gardens, and playground design benefit children physically, go to www .whitehutchinson.com/children/playgroundexp.shtml. Visit the site to learn what other wonderful school settings, such as BellaBoo's Children's Garden in Crown Point, Indiana, are doing to promote and support children's health.

- As children step into the natural world, their creativity and imagination heighten, and their ability to play and converse cooperatively becomes more distinct (Keeler 2008).

- The outdoors is a more robust and effective setting for learning and development than a classroom with four walls (Keeler 2008).

- Nature encourages children to engage and interact with one another (Keeler 2008). As children engage in nature activities, such as playing hide-and-seek amid trees and bushes or making mud pies, they negotiate and compromise among themselves: "This tree is base, okay?" "Let's add sprinkles [sand] to our pies."

My hope is that as you read *Nature Sparks*, you will be inspired by ideas and activities that connect and reclaim nature in children's lives, to enhance not only their academic experiences, but also their health, growth, and development—regardless of individual learning style, culture, economic status, or environmental conditions.

. . . .

Why Bring Out the Nature Lover in a Child?

Where do I start? Discovery, exploration, hands-on experience, observation, appreciation, and recreation—to name just a few. Nature directly and positively complements a child's learning processes and well-being. Traditional and conventional classroom learning largely targets the verbal/linguistic and logical/ mathematical intelligence. Nature is equipped for every child's learning style. It *naturally* extends the learning process in all academic areas, while it allows for greater understanding and deeper insight. A classroom simply cannot duplicate the firsthand observation and learning possibilities in nature. The fresh air and brilliant setting alone are unmatchable. In nature, "school" is literally anywhere!

Giving children experiences in nature and encouraging their interests will benefit them for their entire lives. Listed below are a handful of additional reasons why bringing out the nature lover in a child is vital.

1. Nature enhances a child's learning style through direct hands-on observation and experience.
    Children more readily absorb information when it is presented with a hands-on approach. This method offers genuine living lessons and opportunities (Tu 2006). An example includes collecting and pressing wildflowers and leaves in a scrapbook and studying their individual patterns and markings. A child's inner intelligence is challenged in nature. The outdoor setting allows a child to intensely evaluate, communicate, and observe findings, all of which hones reading, math, and science skills (Keeler 2008).

2. Nature complements the curriculum.
    Friedrich Froebel, an early childhood educator and the father of kindergarten, used nature as a key curriculum component to complement his lessons (Rettig 2005). When teachers integrate nature curriculum, a child is challenged cognitively, and classroom lessons are developmentally enhanced with little effort (Tu 2006). Important scientific skills such as "wondering, questioning, exploring and investigating, discussing, reflecting, and formulating ideas and theories" are honed in nature (Chalufour and Worth 2003, 4). By merely stepping outdoors, children can observe weather patterns, compare elements, sort specimens, categorize earthen textures, and inspect insects. In other words, learn! Nature is definitely its own curriculum.

3. Nature connects children to abstract concepts and assists teachers in instructing them.
    Unfortunately, abstract concepts in classrooms are often words without meaning. Nature acts as a springboard for teachers to bring meaning to abstract classroom concepts. Let's look at an example for clarity. Mrs. Reed's first-grade class is studying the differences and similarities of dirt, sand, and mud. Her class would connect more to their differences and similarities if they ventured to a nearby park and collected samples of each and then tested, charted, and discussed the results. The three elements of nature would just be plain ol' ordinary dirt, sand, and mud if left to merely

reading about the textures in a book. Using nature activities to recreate what is studied in the classroom, children can better relate to and learn abstract concepts.

4. Nature encourages children to be more physically, mentally, and emotionally fit.

   Nature not only stimulates and promotes play and learning, but also contributes to the overall health of children in many areas. It allows them to use their environment for healthy social-emotional, linguistic, physical, and cognitive challenges without even realizing it. Every time they climb a tree, jump a fence, or roll down a hill, their bodies, minds, and spirits are exercised. Nature helps children relax, problem solve, release built-up anxiety and energy, clear their thoughts, gain perspective on things, and sort out inner dilemmas. Allowing time for free play outdoors is an excellent way to encourage children's physical, emotional, cognitive, and social growth. In addition, evidence suggests nature improves the psychological aspect of a child's health (National Environmental Education Foundation 2011).

5. Nature provides opportunities for children to develop an appreciation and awareness of the world around them.

   Acquiring things, raising test scores, and getting to preparatory lessons seem to be the focus of many children's lives, rather than learning to appreciate the beauty and importance of the natural world. Take the time with your students to enjoy and appreciate the fine details of nature. It is a priceless gift! When nature is used as a teaching tool, it allows children to understand their environment as well as real problems within it, such as pollution and energy shortage. Using hands-on class activities such as recycling, composting, encouraging "green" consumption, planting trees and flowers, and enforcing no littering are worthwhile endeavors to demonstrate nature's value and a commitment to protect the natural world and its environment.

. . . .

Is My Child a Naturalist Already?

Like Luca, a child who is a naturalist enjoys nature and loves being outside. Okay. But don't most children prefer being in the outdoors to a classroom? Here are ten common characteristics of a child who is a naturalist:

1. The child harbors an ongoing thirst to play, discover, and explore in the outdoors.

2. The child exhibits strong sensory skills of sight, sound, smell, taste, and touch.

3. The child displays a keen sense of detail, especially to patterns in nature, such as those on leaf tops, turtle shells, or tree trunks.

4. The child demonstrates a natural and loving connection to animals.

5. The child enjoys collecting things in nature.

6. The child is most tranquil when outside. There is a noticeable difference in behavior and attitude when the child is in the classroom as opposed to outdoors.

7. The child relates easily to the outside world. Activities such as camping and hiking come naturally.

8. The child displays a fearless attitude in nature. This might include being unafraid of bugs, worms, snails, beehives, or other intriguing items in nature. She is not timid about climbing high, tracking long, or trudging through smelly, murky mud to marvel at a fiddler crab.

9. The child derives great pleasure from watching videos and reading books about nature and animals.

10. The child enjoys working with and manipulating elements of nature, such as mud, sand, sap, and moss.

As you ponder the list, please keep in mind that whether a child is "naturally" attuned to nature or not, connecting him to nature will greatly benefit his overall development and growth. Here are a few more questions to consider:

- Is the child an intense outdoors observer? This might include reading the sky—monitoring cloud shapes and movements or watching birds fly.

- Does the child enjoy using scientific equipment—such as telescopes, microscopes, and binoculars—to play and observe nature?

- Is the child skilled in, or does she find interest in, categorizing species of plants and animals?

- Is the child concerned about or interested in recycling or other environmental matters?

- Does the child enjoy researching and reading about nature discoveries?

- Is the child very compassionate and sensitive toward creatures, the environment, and natural formations?

How to Get the Most Out of This Book

Nature Sparks is filled with activities, ideas, and tips to connect you and your students to nature, and each chapter offers up useful strategies and resources to bring out a child's inner nature lover. Understanding the way each child best learns and retains information will make it much easier to connect her to the natural world. Once you accomplish this, you'll want to gauge how the child relates to the natural world and if her outdoor interest level is hot—"Let's go find out!"—or cold—"Yuck! I'm not touching that!"

Additionally, *Nature Sparks* presents an array of creative and sensory-integrated sidebar suggestions referred to as "Nature Sparks." A Nature Spark may recommend a connecting storybook that enhances a concept, a list of culminating activities, a craft idea, or a simple mini lesson on a particular subject. Anything triggering academic or sensory extensions to nature may show up as a Nature Spark. Here is a sample Nature Spark:

Nature Spark

When working outdoors with young children, consider their attention spans. Break up activities into manageable chunks of time. Expect a child to pay attention for the number of minutes based on his or her age—for example, five minutes for a five-year-old. Where the natural setting is more stimulating, the time may vary, but this is a good guideline.

The passion for nature you ignite in your students will affect them for a lifetime, whether you feel completely competent about teaching in the outdoors or not. *Nature Sparks* can build on student interests and prompt parental involvement, so share goings-on in newsletters you send home. As sparks fly outdoors, remember your end goal: that children be equipped to understand, connect, and observe the power and beauty of nature in an ever-changing world, even if nature loving does not come naturally.

. . . .

Let's Go!

As you venture through *Nature Sparks*, you will notice an emphasis on nature activities in particular curriculum areas, such as language and literacy, science, art, and multisensory play. Make sure to accommodate students' individual intelligences, interests, and understandings so that all children can engage in the learning. When using nature to teach and learn, you will quickly discover that children work smarter, not harder, and in a shorter amount of time. A more nature-oriented classroom and curriculum foster a child's development largely by using his curiosity and exploration as a catalyst.

Throughout the book I refer often to having students write, reflect, paste, and sketch items in a nature journal. You will find through their use that nature journals are an important learning tool, as is a nature word wall. If possible, erect a nature word wall in the classroom, or use a separate notebook, for newly discovered nature words and drawings to accompany them. Young children who are offered challenging words such as *topsoil* or *erosion*, for example, will develop a richer vocabulary. Do not be leery of offering correct terminology; children do not know the words are "big" and difficult unless you make them out to be.

I hope this book supports and guides your lesson plans toward nature as well as enriches young minds—whether budding naturalists or not. Now grab *your* nature journal and get ready to explore. Bring out your nature lover—it is the first step in bringing out a child's. Let's go!

1

Why is it that some children try new things with enthusiasm and approach peers and adults with confidence, whereas other children seem to believe that they are incapable in many situations? . . . What can we learn from research that will allow us to help children approach new situations with confidence?

—H. H. Marshall

Bringing All Children Closer to Nature

The outdoors should not be considered a place for children to merely run off steam, but rather as an extension of the classroom—an additional and equal place to develop social, emotional, cognitive, and physical skills (Odoy and Foster 1997). Incorporating a creative and hands-on, nature-based education for young children involves preparation, thought, and concept planning well beyond the ABCs and 123s. Teaching young children about their natural environment within their natural environment is challenging and rewarding work that fosters one of the most vital ingredients for effective learning—wonderment. Rachel Carson expressed it well in her book *The Sense of Wonder* (1956, 56): "It is not half so important to know as to feel. . . . The years of early childhood are the time to prepare the soil."

Realistically, though, not all children are eager to study the natural environment. Think of the child who dares not get her hands or clothes dirty. What about the feisty child who would rather fiddle with an electronic toy than climb a tree? Although my experiences as an educator have led me to believe that most children enjoy being outdoors, for some children the words, "Come quickly! Look at this cool bug!" are just jumbled words of nonsense—the children simply are not interested. Whether this stems from a personal lack of interest, a stifling urban school environment, or a home life that does not encourage outdoor interaction, bringing *all* children closer to nature is possible. There is almost always a moment in the day to explore the natural world with children in subtle, meaningful ways, even if just to "lure the little ones to come to a window and notice light raindrops, driving rain, the delicate shapes of snowflakes" (Honig 2004, 22). Nature is full of wondrous teachable moments that are nearly impossible to dodge. As educators and child care professionals, we need to take advantage of and nurture such learning opportunities.

With this in mind, remember that bringing out a child's inner nature lover does not mean forcing dramatic changes—a tactic that probably will not work and may backfire, causing the child to retreat. Keep an eye out for the rarity, for unpredictability, and for unusualness within nature to connect a child to it. These are the things that intrigue children (Talbot and Frost 1989).

Remember, too, that children who develop a sense of respect and care for nature in their early childhood years are inclined to grow to appreciate the natural world as adults. Strive to instill, deep in their hearts, seeds of nature appreciation, awareness, and awe. Accomplish this not only by providing nature activities and instructional strategies, but also by modeling passion for the environment. Passion for the outdoors is contagious!

Finally, remember that children who have ample opportunities for direct sensory experiences and positive peer interactions with the natural world learn and develop better than those who are not allowed such conditions. Strive to use nature-oriented learning techniques to enhance student development and life quality (Woyke 2004).

When you focus on these three points, you will quickly discover that effectively integrating nature into the curriculum creates an atmosphere where students may thrive in many developmental areas:

- creativity

- self-confidence

- self-discipline

- observation

- social interaction
- literacy and language
- problem solving

. . . .

Use Nature to Heighten a Child's Sensory Awareness

Heightening a child's sensory awareness implies improving his ability to use each sense—hearing, seeing, touching, and smelling—to more closely observe and discriminate details and concepts. It also promotes a child's ability to appreciate beauty, express creativity, and perceive patterns (Torquati and Barber 2005). When children develop strong sensory skills, they become more aware of them in a variety of settings.

Nature is best understood through exploration, observation, discovery, and attention to details that are stimulated by the senses. A child's sense of touch can be heightened in nature by taking him on a blindfolded nature walk where he is asked to feel and respond specifically to specimens of nature. Using nature to heighten sensory awareness can broaden a variety of learning areas, such as literacy, problem solving, and observation. Use alphabet scavenger hunts, nature excursions, sensory trails, and several other novel ideas to do it!

Alphabet Scavenger Hunt: An alphabet scavenger hunt combines observation and literacy skills, because children have to spell and select suitable words when they play. The game is easy once the rules are explained and modeled. First, have students write the alphabet in their nature journals with a marker; this may take up several pages. Next to each letter have the children write down and/or draw an object that correctly corresponds with the letter. Students can work in pairs or alone. Here is a brief sample list (Hammerman, Hammerman, and Hammerman 2001).

A—ant	**D**—dirt	**G**—gravel
B—bird	**E**—earthworm	
C—cloud	**F**—fall leaves	

An alphabet scavenger hunt can be easily modified when it is focused on a shape, color, or single letter. Refer to the two following examples:

Color Hunt: Red	Letter Hunt: B
A—apple core	Bryan, my classmate
B—brick on school building	bushes on the playground
C—coat on step	bicycles across the street
D—drink can in recycling bin	bark on a tree

For successful hunts, work with children's interests as well as their motivation to learn. Two wonderful books provide introductory activities: *Amazon Alphabet* by Martin and Tanis Jordon and *Roger Tory Peterson's ABC of Birds: A Book for Little Birdwatchers* by Linda Westervelt. Both books are beautifully illustrated and will captivate children as they learn the alphabet. An added bonus: the use of alphabet books promotes phonological awareness!

Nature Excursions: Another activity to develop a child's sensory awareness is a nature excursion. Two types of excursions that are useful to lure children into the natural world are observation excursions and experience excursions. Excursions are meant to stimulate a child's individual senses. Let's quickly review each sense as applicable to observation and experience excursions (Hammerman, Hammerman, and Hammerman 2001):

- Sight: When on excursions, have children notice colors, shapes, sizes, and forms in nature. Have students look for a variety of birds in the sky and slimy slugs and bugs on the ground. Offer magnifying glasses and other nature tools to assist in focusing their attention by using their eyes. Ask sight-prompting questions, such as "What do you see?" or "What can you tell me about it?" Make sure the questions are specific.

- Hearing: Have children listen for noises and decide whether they are loud or soft. Compare and contrast natural sounds (such as animals) and man-made sounds (such as machines). Have students close their eyes. (Young children can be "peekers," so use blindfolds.) Ask questions that

Nature Spark

Inform children if they come across an ant colony while on a nature hunt to remain several feet away from it. The same goes for unfamiliar nests, holes, or bushes. Bushes often house biting insects. Offer binoculars and demonstrate how to use them so children can watch ant mounds and beehives up close (Arnosky 2002).

focus on hearing, such as "What do you hear?" and "How do the birds sound?"

- Smell: Allow children to sniff natural fragrances, such as freshly cut grass, fall leaves, or wildflowers. Have children crush nature items in their hands and smell the outcome. Ask prompting questions related to smelling, such as "What does that smell like?" and "Have you smelled it before?"

- Touch: Ask children to feel nature items that are soft, hard, smooth, and rough. Have children stand in the wind and feel it with their whole body. Have them lie in the grass on a warm afternoon and feel the sun's heat on their face. Ask touch questions, such as "What does that feel like?" or "How does it feel on your skin?"

- Taste: Stimulating the sense of taste will need to take place in the classroom. Tasting nature specimens is dangerous. Speak with students about this issue. Collect a variety of salty, sweet, bitter, and sour items for children to explore with their taste buds. Ask prompting taste questions: "Does it taste good? Bad?" or "What kind of face do you think you will make when you taste it?" (Humphryes 2000).

Nature excursions are fun and educational for children of all ages. They nurture wonderment. For an *observation excursion*, take children out to the playground or backyard and ask them to focus on one item in nature—a bird, for example—for several minutes using one of their senses. Set a timer. Ask follow-up questions when the timer goes off, such as "How do you know birds are alive? Where do they live? What do they eat? How do you know?"

Another way to hone sensory skills is an *experience excursion*. Experience excursions involve direct physical contact with nature. Start an experience excursion by having children lie on the grass to feel the sun in their face and the prickly grass at their backs. Have students then move to a shaded spot and discuss the differences in what they see and feel.

Outdoor excursions are beneficial because they give children the opportunity to become comfortable with the outdoor setting, making it easier for them to learn from it (Humphryes 2000). Writing, drawing, and art lessons generated from nature excursions are limitless. Additional resources to encourage the development of a child's sensory awareness are available in the appendix.

Nature Spark

When venturing out in tall grass, weeds, or wildflowers, be sure to have students tuck their pants into their socks to prevent bites and the "itchies." Apply sunscreen and insect repellent if out and about in the elements for a while.

Make authentic-looking maps for students to carry on their sensory trails or scavenger hunts. Cut map-sized pieces from brown paper bags. Draw the map markings or directions with permanent marker. Burn the ends and wipe down the map with olive oil or coffee for an old and tattered look.

Sensory Awareness Trails: A sensory awareness trail features stations that allow children to fine-tune their senses. On sensory awareness trails, students are paired up and must work as a team. Work on a sensory awareness trail will require nature journals and supplies, such as markers, pencils, paper, and a well-illustrated map, which can be carried in a "nature bag." Stations should be labeled clearly on the map. A mock run-through will allow you to discuss each station and the steps taken there. A sensory trail can be simple or detailed. Be sure to consider age appropriateness.

Below is an example of a sensory awareness trail with three stations. Use words and pictures for emerging readers. Pictures only will suffice for nonreaders. Nonreaders will need an adult chaperone at each station to ensure the station work is completed correctly.

Station 1: Tree Stop

One student may say to the other:

- Remove a leaf from the tree. Smell the leaf. How does it smell? Crush the leaf in your hand. Smell it. How does it smell?

- Pick a wildflower next to the tree. How does it smell? Draw the wildflower in your nature journal.

- With the tape in your nature bag, attach a piece of paper to the tree. Rub a crayon or pencil over the tree bark until you see the bark's outline.

Station 2: Picnic Table

One student may say to the other:

- On a picnic table by the swings, you will discover a snail shell. Look at it closely and notice its colors and patterns. Sketch the snail shell in your nature journal.

- Look at the inside of the snail shell and the outside. How are they alike? How are they different?

- Using natural clay, roll a snail shell. Using colored aquarium pebbles, create a pattern on the outside.

Station 3: Tree Hole

One student may say to the other:

- Look at the hole in the tree. What type of animal do you think might live inside? Why?

Nature Spark

Here's a quick activity to incorporate as children study trees and birds. Help students decorate a tree with colored strips of string, fabric scraps, dryer lint, stuffing from old furniture, and cotton balls. Watch together as birds gather the materials to build nests. See if you can find any colorful nests around the playground or neighborhood.

- Why do you think the animal picked this tree? What do you think it eats?

- In your nature journal, draw the animal you think lives in the tree hole (Hammerman, Hammerman, and Hammerman 2001).

Note to teacher or parent volunteer: On each child's trail map, denote a final station for reflection through drawing, painting, block building, or writing. Chapters 2 and 3 present special places for children to relax and reflect after activities. Play music in the background.

To make nature hunts, excursions, and trails meaningful and exciting for students, think back to your own childhood memories. Additionally, nature experiences can be used in future classroom activities. Turn flower petals, collected on an excursion, into potpourri (art and science) or use them in a sorting activity (math). Encourage students to use and enjoy all their senses appropriately while in nature. When children are able to appreciate each sense, a whole new way of looking at the natural world is made available to them.

. . . .

Use Nature to Develop Social, Literacy, and Language Skills

Nature provides continuous opportunities to challenge a child's play (Torquati and Barber 2005), and the endless sensory experiences it offers can teach and refine early learning proficiencies, including social, literacy, and language skills as well as play development. The following activities explore social skills and literacy and language skills, and they build ideas and strategies to bring children closer to nature and foster a sense of wonder.

Social Skills

Nature is a wonderful location for developing problem-solving and social skills. It is full of problem-solving endeavors that students must negotiate. As children explore nature, they interact with each other, sharing and discussing curiosities as well as compromising over differences. Outdoor prop boxes and Big Jobs encourage social play and can help bring children closer to nature.

OUTDOOR PROP BOXES

Playing with peers enhances children's learning and helps them develop feelings of competence (Drew and Rankin 2004). Social skills are inevitably nurtured as children play together in the outdoors. Laced with dramatic play, the social outlet widens. Through dramatic play, children interact, share, take turns, role-play, practice literacy and language skills, and expand their understandings of the world around them (Myhre 1993). Regardless of place, a dramatic play area offers children opportunities to be successful, self-directing social players.

To bring students closer to the natural world, allow their imaginations to be exercised by expanding a dramatic play area outdoors with the use of play prop boxes. An outdoor prop box is full of themed items to generate and expand dramatic play anywhere. As you prepare prop boxes, thoroughly consider the purpose of each box, as well as age appropriateness and safety guidelines. For example, a repair-shop prop box may allow children to explore a variety of old appliances, which reinforces problem solving, fine motor skills, and social skills. As students tinker with discarded gadgets, they'll problem solve and generate social conversations—"Look at the wheels inside this VCR! What did you find? What does the inside of yours look like?"—without even trying. Make sure that tools, such as screwdrivers, are age appropriate, and discuss safety guidelines for the repair shop.

To gather, organize, and facilitate neat and orderly prop boxes, call a local copy or office supply store. Ask them to save their empty computer-paper boxes for you. Plastic crates may also be used. Although cardboard boxes are not as durable as plastic crates, sturdy computer boxes are easy to store, label, and replace. In the class newsletter, ask parents for items. Call stores directly. For example, call a hair salon for contributions of small combs, empty shampoo bottles, aprons, and wigs for a hair-salon prop box (Myhre 1993). Contact hardware stores, lock-and-key shops, tile shops, construction sites, and hospitals for the following prop-box items (Ross 2000):

- discarded locks and keys
- plastic tubs
- PVC pipes and acrylic tubing

- plastic tweezers
- a variety of squeeze bottles
- funnels
- pulleys and plungers
- trowels

Flower Shop: A flower-shop prop box can be easily and beautifully situated in a garden or outdoor play place, such as a sand or dirt area. Fill the prop box with paper, tissue, plastic, or real flowers. To make the area more aesthetically appealing, plant a variety of annuals or herb plants in unusual containers, such as wagons or old drawers. (Be sure to drill or hammer drainage holes in homemade flowerpots.) Here are props to put in the flower-shop prop box:

- used garden magazines and books
- child-sized garden tools
- brightly colored floral aprons
- garden hats, bonnets, and gloves
- empty watering cans of all shapes and sizes (plastic and metal)
- empty seed packets
- a variety of flower vases and baskets
- a cash register and play money

Bakery: An outdoor bakery prop box is a wonderful way to expand mud-pie making and sand-cake baking. Leave it on a small log or step stool for children to find. For the bakery prop box, mix up a variety of earthen "soups and sauces" and place them in large gallon containers with sturdy lids. An example of an earthen soup might include sand mixed with small pebbles, lots of water, and squishy plastic worms. Flower petals and crushed leaves can become instant spices for bakery menus. Use old oven racks as a cooling station for freshly baked goods. Fill a recipe-card box with colorful index cards to encourage recipe writing. Other props for a bakery box include the following:

- cookie sheets
- measuring cups of all sizes

Nature Spark

A bakery-play prop box will not only allow children to bake dirt cakes and pour mucky purees, but also to experiment with textures and other science concepts, such as absorption, evaporation, and permeability. A bakery prop box can lead to endless imaginative play. Ask students to create a seven-course mud meal to serve to each other—and you!

- handheld mixers with the cord cut off
- cake pans of all sorts, shapes, and sizes—(Bundt, 13" x 9" rectangular, and loaf)
- oven mitts and aprons
- rolling pins
- pots and pans of all shapes and sizes
- clean, empty milk cartons
- plastic and wooden kitchen utensils
- aluminum foil and paper cups
- toss-ins for baking "garnish" (see page 115)
- cash register and play money

Veterinarian's Clinic: Finally a use for all those toy animal collections! Send a note home to parents asking for contributions. Use a vet-clinic prop box to introduce famous naturalists such as Dian Fossey, who was dedicated to the conservation and protection of gorillas and their habitats (include several large gorillas). Rotate a variety of animals through the prop box. Give it a weekly theme—cat care one week, followed by large cat care (lions and tigers) the next. Additional props for a veterinary-clinic box might include the following:

- small rolls of cloth bandages
- a variety of tape
- eyedroppers
- cotton balls and tips
- stethoscopes
- old pet carriers
- animal combs and brushes
- sponges of all sizes
- rubber gloves
- clipboards
- smocks

Repair Shop: Children enjoy taking apart appliances! Old circuit boards and gears with colored wires and gizmos are science investigations at their best. An outdoor repair-shop prop box

Nature Spark

A repair-shop prop box is magnificent for enhancing problem-solving and scientific-investigating skills. The prop box is also a wonderful introduction to studying pulleys, springs, levers, and magnets. As children tinker with discarded VCRs, tape players, CB radios, disc players—even TVs with their screens removed—they will wonder why the gadget broke, how it might be fixed, or what it might be turned into. It's also helpful to little hands if the screws are loosened.

stocked with an assortment of intriguing gadgets, magnets, and more will spark children's desire to wonder and fiddle. Recommended items include alarm clocks, irons, hand vacuums, radios, and toasters. Make sure to cut off cords and tape accordingly. This prop box could be set up at a picnic table or in an open grassy area. Insist that children wear safety hats and goggles, regardless of what they are working on, to reinforce the safety factor. Small Phillips and flat-head screwdrivers, pliers, nails, and hammers can be sharp, and plywood can be splintery, so enforce and be consistent with repair-shop safety rules. Other items to place in the repair-shop prop box include the following:

- several measuring tapes
- pencils
- building blueprints
- calculators
- wrenches
- plastic hard hats
- gloves
- nuts and bolts
- scrap wood

Nature Spark

Although architects and designers have not used blueprints in years, a quick call to a local construction site for any archived donations is a possibility. A newsletter to parents is also an option. You never know what may turn up.

Outdoor Grocery Market: An outdoor produce stand or grocery market is a perfect prop-box idea, especially when displayed in a mini play orchard (see page 81). Fresh vegetables and fruit can be used as well as plastic versions. Fill empty boxes and containers with real food items, such as macaroni or rice, for sound and weight. Collect egg cartons, two-liter bottles, and other items. Ask a local grocery store to donate brown paper bags. Set up shelves using crates and plywood to display a food scale. Set out small note cards or colored dot stickers for pricing items. If possible, situate outdoor market shelves in a way that hones classification skills by categorizing foods. Additional grocery-market prop-box items include the following:

- toy grocery cart
- empty food containers and boxes
- an assortment of small baskets

- a cash register with pretend money

- adding machine with the paper tape included

- telephone with message pad

Camping: A camping prop box can be perfect outdoor play for spring or early fall. Spark imaginative camping adventures by setting up lawn furniture. Display child-sized fishing poles with tackle boxes full of plastic worms and play bait. Make magnetic fishing poles for children to use. Place metal on the end of the poles in place of the hook. Create a play pond full of fabric or foam fish with magnetic pieces attached. Pitch a small tent and throw several sleeping bags inside. Ignite a pretend campfire. Set out paper plates, plastic silverware, and a frying pan. For a treat, teachers can supervise children as they "roast" marshmallows over a heated Bunsen burner or hot plate. Other camping prop-box ideas include the following:

- plastic foods

- a tin or metal coffeepot with mugs

- thermos

- pots and pans

- small cooler full of empty bottles

- sunglasses

- binoculars

- flashlight

Other outdoor dramatic-play prop-box ideas include the following:

- a dentist office

- a zookeeper

- a kennel keeper

- a dog groomer

- a post office

- a pet shop owner

- an outdoor tea party

- a farm and ranch hand

- an outdoor theater

- a spaceship
- a park ranger station
- a police or fire station
- a doctor's office or nurse's station

Be sure to fill boxes with age-appropriate picture books related to the prop-box theme for children to explore. Regardless of the theme, keep prop-box supplies diverse and versatile. Prop boxes can be as simple as a bubble-blowing bonanza, complete with a variety of wands and buckets, or something more intense, such as an outdoor painter's studio situated on a deck or playground patio. For painting prop boxes, rotate paint supply continually. Children will enjoy experimenting with many colors, such as baby-blue and sky-blue, as well as many shades of red, orange, yellow, and green. Use a variety of paint palettes, such as muffin tin pans or old plastic plates. Offer a variety of hats and aprons for children to don as artists. The objective of any dramatic-play prop box is to extend individual interests without changing the overall theme. Prop boxes can be extended to outdoor special spaces, as discussed in chapter 3.

COOPERATIVE BIG JOBS

Complex learning takes place when children work and play cooperatively outdoors. Children grow emotionally when allowed to participate in purposeful, physical activities that challenge their problem-solving, social, and physical skills (Jones 2005). Outdoor nature-learning experiences are richer when children bump into challenging academic boundaries and experience hearty, whole-body workouts. The use of Big Jobs allows such an experience. What's a Big Job? Simply put, a Big Job is a large task requiring several children to complete it (Jones 2005). Students must work as a team to complete a Big Job. The creative use of Big Job group size and arrangement encourages positive social and emotional growth in children—"My classmates need my help! My teacher is relying on *me!*"

Big Jobs nurture "*effectance motivation*—the desire to solve challenging problems for the gratification of discovering a solution—and its key components" (Jones 2005, 87). In addition to bringing children closer to nature, Big Jobs allow educators the opportunity to provide meaningful nature-oriented activities and employ nature-oriented instructional strategies, which build student confidence and success in and out of the classroom. Research supports the use of Big Jobs to challenge children and shows that completing a Big Job prepares children to take on new challenges with feelings of confidence and competence (Jones 2005). Big Jobs require children to practice the following skills:

- identifying a problem or task that requires a resolution
- planning and mapping out a solution
- working physically (often breaking a sweat)
- collaborating
- following directions
- negotiating
- compromising

Children need proper tools to complete Big Jobs, and they need to be properly supervised, especially with small tools such as hammers, nails, and screwdrivers. Big Jobs require rules and guidelines for safe and proper tool storage. A Big Job tool list for children might consist of the following:

- child-sized brooms and mops (including push brooms and whisk mops)
- dustpans
- different-sized sponges
- a variety of plastic buckets
- real child-sized outdoor equipment, such as plastic and metal rakes and hoes, wagons, and carts
- crates
- watering cans
- snow shovels

Through Big Jobs, children will discover they can make a difference (Jones 2005). Listed below are Big Jobs that can be incorporated into a daily schedule. Please consider age appropriateness and season with each suggestion.

Playground Cleanup: A playground is always in need of tidying up. Whether picking up scattered debris after a blustery rainstorm or sweeping an asphalt area after an afternoon of mighty sand play, the playground is full of Big Job possibilities. With students, write up a list of playground tasks that need to be completed and check them off as accomplished. A playground cleanup project list might include the following:

- replacing wood chips in the swings area

- reorganizing, sorting, and returning outdoor toys to their bin

- cleaning toys in pails of sudsy water

- sweeping the patio with a variety of brooms and mops

Allow students to transport the water pails from the water spigot to their Big Job working spot. Students will benefit from the physical work!

Table Cleanup: Cleaning messy water, mud, or sensory tables is a hearty Big Job. Assist children as they tote the tables outdoors for hosing and scrubbing down. Have students work together to unwind the hose, as well as to rewind it when done. If a hose is not available, use water buckets and a variety of large sponges and brushes. Give the table a more creative kick after cleaning by adding nature specimens and new toys.

Garden Cleanup: Cleaning up a garden area after a long winter can be a productive and worthwhile Big Job. Children will learn to appreciate the gardening process and the steps involved in making a spring garden flourish. The tasks involved in a garden cleanup Big Job are abundant: pulling and bagging dead leaves and weeds, putting the bagged remains in the school Dumpster, turning over the soil and adding mulch, and planting new seeds in the garden area. You will definitely need to replace gardening gloves after this big garden cleanup!

Leaf Patrol: Children should have lots of opportunities to play in big piles of crisp and colorful leaves. Fall presents a traditional childhood Big Job—raking crunchy leaves. A leaf-patrolling Big Job has simple and enjoyable steps.

1. Rake fallen leaves into a pile.

2. Jump in leaves.

3. Repeat steps 1 and 2 several times.

4. Rerake leaves and stuff in big bags.

5. Lug leaf bags to school Dumpster and discard.

Every child should have the opportunity and pleasure of taking on a leaf-patrolling Big Job.

Nature Spark

Gardens nurture many skills:

Science: observe plants as they grow from seeds and respond to sun and water.

Literacy: learn the names of plants, read books about plants, and write nature journal responses.

Math: count seeds, compare sizes, chart plant growth, and record rainfall.

Social: bring children together and possibly involve the community.

Snow Shoveling: Shoveling snow from a walkway with child-sized snow shovels is a Big Job guaranteed to flush faces, make cheeks rosy, and exercise little bodies. Have children clear snow-covered paths so they can ride tricycles or push wagons on the asphalt. Have students also shovel slush. Have children write in their nature journals about the differences between slush and snow. Serve hot cocoa after completing a snow-shoveling Big Job. Read *The Snowy Day* by Ezra Jack Keats.

Pet Cleanup: If you have critters in your classroom, children can clean and scrub out cages, aquariums, or small containers. Take the animal homes outdoors so they can be hosed down, or clean them in the classroom on a large tarp with textured towels and sudsy water. Implementing a regularly scheduled pet cleanup can instill responsibility in students.

Plant Care: Tending to classroom plants is a Big Job that can be broken down into small steps. Plants need to be watered, pruned, and repotted. Repotting can be done outdoors or indoors. Allow students to gather all repotting supplies, such as soil and trowels, and ask them to work as a team replanting greenery into larger pots. See page 34 for additional container plant ideas. Students can plant and monitor a variety of herb gardens or annual flower beds. Record the growth of herbs and annuals growing in pots indoors versus in beds outdoors. Compare and contrast the results. Discuss similarities and differences. Additional examples of questions to ask about outdoor plant growth and care include the following:

- Do shaded outdoor plants turn toward the light?

- Do roots change direction to find water (plant in transparent plastic containers)?

- If an outdoor plant's stem is cut, can it survive outdoors? Indoors?

Nature Spark

Hang child-friendly plants—such as aloe, bamboo, cast-iron plant, Christmas cactus, pothos, and spider plant—from the ceiling, or put them on shelves and on window ledges. Make sure they are not situated too close to classroom heating or cooling sources.

Literacy and Language Skills

Over the past decade, the demand has grown for new and effective teaching strategies that meet children's diverse literacy and language needs (Hill-Clarke and Robinson 2004). Nature laced with music and art, for example, can creatively develop literacy and language skills and meet individualized learning needs. By providing open-ended nature activities in areas such as dramatic play, literature, and large-muscle movement, literacy and language can be expanded beyond simple, everyday reading and writing tasks.

INTERACTIVE STORYTELLING

A literacy- and language-rich environment with a balance of reading, writing, speaking, and listening activities is important for effective early childhood learning. Interactive storytelling enhances creative expression, listening skills, and vocabulary. Bring children to nature through interactive storytelling. Combine storytelling with beautifully illustrated nature books and props. Not only will literacy skills flourish, but children will be lured to the natural world. Use the following five steps to carry out effective interactive storytelling that features nature.

1. Choose an age-appropriate book. Make sure it has several characters and a sequential plot, such as Eric Carle's *The Grouchy Ladybug* and *The Very Hungry Caterpillar*. Additional interactive storybook suggestions can be found in the appendix.

2. Ask students to predict what the story might be about by showing the cover and reading the title aloud. Leaf through the book briefly, showing random pages to the children.

3. Introduce the story's main characters. List them on chart paper or a flannel board and assign characters that children can act out. Nature-oriented props include fall leaves to crumble, a dried gourd to rattle, and a bag of pebbles to shake.

4. Before reading the book, give volunteers the props so they can practice their roles. After a few practice rounds, read the story out loud with enthusiasm and inflection. Emphasize each character.

5. Finish the story with a discussion. Ask students about the story's setting, plot, and ending. Ask students what other props could be used. Then have students draw their favorite character in their nature journal, as well as write about why it was a favorite (Hill-Clarke and Robinson 2004).

Nature Spark

Bernard Waber's *Bearsie Bear and the Surprise Sleepover Party* is a great interactive storybook that plays with sounds and letters. Children will marvel at the characters—Moosie Moose, Foxie Fox, Goosie Goose, and others. Such stories are wonderful for allowing children to predict and add silly sounds and vibrant props to represent each character (Yopp and Yopp 2009).

Nature Spark

Set out cloth story bags filled with props, such as puppets, figurines, feathers, and other creative items children can use to invent stories.

Books that play with sounds, alliteration, and rhyming are highly recommended for interactive storytelling. Examples include *Cock-a-Doodle-Moo!* by Bernard Most. In this delightful story, children are exposed to a variety of mixed-up ways a rooster attempts to crow "Cock-a-doodle-doo!" including "Mock-a-moodle-moo!" and "Sock-a-noodle-moo!" What fun! Preview interactive storybooks before reading them to children. Avoid books with stereotypical themes or messages.

Nature Charades: An imaginative round of nature charades fosters creative expression and literacy skills as well as physical movement. Nature charades can be embellished with colorful props, such as scarves, ribbons, clip art mounted on craft sticks, bells, and boas. The props are meant to provide a concrete way to introduce students to words they will hear in the story. Storybooks can also be turned into creative charades. Use the following steps to play nature charades:

1. Display a variety of nature words: *summer*, *rainbow*, *bug*, or *flower*, for example. If possible, write the words on large sheets of chart paper. Add pictures and laminate. Children will enjoy circling words and letters with dry-erase markers after the game is played.

2. Read each word aloud enthusiastically to students.

3. Using movement and a variety of props, allow a student to act out a word from the list while the other students guess which word it is. An example you might demonstrate for *rainbow* is waving several colored silk scarves back and forth in the air. For *bug*, click and clack a castanet on the floor using your fingers. Other prop ideas include egg shakers (plastic eggs filled with beans or rice and sealed with hot glue), soap bubbles, colored flags, rhythm sticks, and dried gourds.

Turn the Latin American folktale "The Elegant Rooster" into a charade or skit. In the story, a rooster is on his way to a wedding when he finds a piece of corn on the ground. The rooster eats the corn but soils his beak in the process. Realizing the problem, he asks his friends—which include the daisy, the sheep, the dog, the stick, and the fire—to help him, but most of them say, "*¡No quiero!* I don't want to!" (Russo, Colurciello, and Kelly 2008). Children can act out the parts of the animals and elements with creative props while others try to guess the storybook characters.

Nature Spark

Encourage motor skills while playing nature charades. Have students use props and movements to express words. And remember, props can be simple—a crepe paper strip attached to a dowel becomes a streamer. Act out phrases, such as "jump in a lake," where children jump in a hula hoop, or "climb a mountain," where children climb over bright orange cones. Make a chart out of the following action words and give it a go:

gallop

creep

tiptoe

balance

stretch

lunge

wiggle

The Mitten by Jan Brett is another story that lends itself to nature charades. In this beautifully illustrated Ukrainian folktale, retold and illustrated by Jan Brett, a variety of animals—such as a mole, rabbit, and badger—come upon a lost mitten. They each squeeze their way inside the warm mitten until a big brown bear and a tiny mouse make their entrances. An unexpected sneeze from one of the animals sends them all flying through the snow. Students can predict which animal's sneeze would be powerful enough to cause such a commotion. Children can re-create the mitten scene by throwing a blanket over a table and crawling under it. Children can also make creative costumes for each animal, then act out the storybook.

Nature Notes: This activity nurtures creative expression, music appreciation, and writing skills. Songs such as Hap Palmer and Martha Cheney's "Scamper"—a cat-and-mouse circle game, which is found on the album *Witches' Brew*—can be read, sung, and dramatized with creativity. Nature notes is a simple activity:

1. Gather a variety of musical selections to play for children outdoors. Possibilities include reggae, country, classical, rhythm and blues, and bluegrass. Be creative in your selections.

2. Have students select a page in their nature journals where they can draw. As you play each tune, ask students to draw what the music reminds them of or what image it brings to their minds.

3. Ask students to share their drawings and the reasoning behind them.

4. Prompt students to notice how the same song can evoke different thoughts and moods in different people.

Sensory Play: Any hands-on sensory play encourages children to converse among themselves, especially if the play is captivating and combined with fresh air and sunshine. For example, an outdoor sensory table filled with cornstarch goop, corn kernels, rice, and shells is guaranteed to get children talking (Kalmar 2008). Have children practice writing their names or sight words in the gunk with craft sticks or small twigs.

Block Building: Block building fosters language and literacy skill acquisition naturally because children have to talk about

building plans. Provide large rolls of paper and pencils to record language, literacy, and social skills (Kalmar 2008). Block building allows children to consult with other "builders," plan, exchange ideas, compromise, and problem solve using words. If moved to an outdoor setting, amid sand, gravel, or dirt mounds full of bugs and rocks, the play and learning potential intensifies.

Dramatic Play: Dramatic play produces instant language exchange as children engage in various roles, rules, and themes (Kalmar 2008). Creative props, such as wedding veils, capes, parasols, headdresses, vests, fancy gloves, receipts, order pads, menus, and pens, stimulate creative conversation for play. "You're the bride, so you'll need to wear the shiny red shoes and the veil. I'll wear the fancy gloves, okay?" Let children make costumes out of large brown paper bags and move to music. Set out a box of fancy boots and shoes to spark long periods of dramatic play. Refer to page 18 where dramatic-play prop boxes are discussed.

Scrapbooking: An outdoor scrapbooking table can spark lively conversation among children. Using clip art, nature artifacts, magazines, or items collected from field trips, set up an attractive area with assorted supplies, such as paint, markers, stamps, ribbons, hole punchers, and other interesting embellishments. Scrapbooking encourages children to discuss and recall events as they build their pages. "Remember when we went to the pumpkin patch and I found the biggest pumpkin?" Children can also turn sections of their nature journals into scrapbook pages.

Entice Children into Nature with Outdoor Gardens

Young children develop academic skills from garden experiences (Rosenow 2008). Offer a smorgasbord of outdoor gardening opportunities by turning a section of your playground into a garden full of vibrant colors, textures, and fragrances. When implementing a gardening project, your objective should be to connect children to the natural world using bugs, plants, flowers, and earthy sensory experiences.

Theme Gardens: Gardens offer wonderful opportunities for curriculum expansion. Incorporating a small theme garden into your daily class schedule will introduce a variety of science concepts and enhance fine- and gross-motor skills. Garden themes are limitless:

- Use sand, fine gravel, cedar chips, and colored stones to create a simple *desert* garden. Let students make artistic patterns out of sand and stone materials. Make lanterns to hang from a line.

- Although prickly, a beautifully colored *rose* garden can teach children valuable planting and pruning lessons. Roses welcome a range of insects and birds for observing.

- A *candy*-theme garden is a novel idea. Fence in the garden with plastic peppermint sticks, which can be purchased on sale after the winter holidays. Plant peppermint, chocolate mint, ginger, and wild cinnamon. Toss cocoa beans around the planted herbs.

- Children will love an *animal*-theme garden. Plant monkey flowers, tiger lilies, buffalo grass, snapdragons, and cat mint. Connect the garden theme to classroom storybooks, art projects, and games. *Caps for Sale: A Tale of a Peddler, Some Monkeys, and Their Monkey Business* by Esphyr Slobodkina is an entertaining story to connect to planting monkey flowers, low-growing flowers that can be planted easily in the shade. Children will enjoy monkey flowers' physical appearance in a cool garden spot. Be sure to research and discuss the reasoning behind its peculiar name.

- Personalize a playground for children with an *alphabet* garden. Plant herbs, flowers, and vegetables that correspond to children's first names. For example, plant peas for Phillip, bluebells for Bella, and tomatoes for Thomas. Let children choose their own plant from an assortment of seeds. Tending to their own plants will give children a sense of ownership (Wilson 1997).

- A simple *butterfly* garden can be implemented using birdbaths surrounded by butterfly-attracting flowers, such as

Nature Spark

Designate a section in students' nature journals for gardening entries. Have students date entries and track the growth of their garden. Children can record their observations and predictions, as well as take photographs of the key stages in their garden projects. A garden journal can also be used to chart rainfall in the garden and animals observed visiting and nibbling at sprouts. Add favorite recipes that use produce (Starbuck and Olthof 2008).

Nature Spark

If students find a chrysalis or cocoon in a butterfly garden, keep and observe it for only a few days and then release it back into the wild.

coneflowers, marigolds, and sunflowers. Attract a variety of flying beauties by situating flowers tallest to shortest (sunflowers in back, marigolds in front). Welcome caterpillars to the garden by planting parsley.

- Grow a *teatime* garden using lemon thyme, spearmint, and sage herbs. Set up a variety of tables and chairs for tea party play amid the garden scents. Set out a teatime prop box full of dress-up clothes, dolls, and dishes in the garden as well.

- Plant radishes, lettuce, spinach, carrots, and bush beans for a produce garden. These plants will do wonderfully in the smallest spaces; they also have a short growing season and require very little maintenance. Diverse stems and leaves will give children opportunities to sort and classify.

As children plan and prepare themed gardening projects, encourage them to use all their senses for observing, playing, and working in the natural setting. If light rain falls while they work, ask, "How does the rain sound?" Other questions include: "How does the wind feel?" or "How do the flowers smell?" or "How does the sand feel compared to dirt?" Torquati and Barber (2005, 45) state, "Open-ended questions and simple statements scaffold children's observations to help them look more deeply and listen more closely."

Herb Gardens: An herb garden is a wonderful way to bring children closer to nature. Herbs such as rosemary, oregano, sage, thyme, lavender, mint, and onion stimulate little noses. An herb garden can be enclosed with white picket fencing and situated easily between play equipment. Plant a variety of herbs within a small patch of other plants, such as alpine strawberries, alfalfa, or pumpkins. Plant a pizza parlor herb garden in a large wooden wagon wheel. Grow oregano, basil, garlic, rosemary, and parsley. Wheat, tomatoes, and peppers are easy extensions for a pizza-parlor garden. Add a prop box full of wonderful accessories, such as dough for making pizzas, to propel play. Add aprons and notepads for taking orders. Set a table and chairs next to the pizza garden pizzeria.

Vegetable or Flower Gardens: Any type of garden reaps rewards as well as opportunities for skill building and problem solving. A small vegetable or flower garden can be planted in

Nature Spark

For teatime garden play, let children make garden hats out of creative supplies. Have a garden party with tea and shortbread.

Nature Spark

Here are two supersimple gardening ideas for urban conditions:

1. Plant a small flower in a clean gallon jar (plastic pickle jars work well). Children can observe leaf and root growth.
2. Plant geraniums or dill seedlings in a small container and set on a windowsill. They will spark the gardening process and, when the windows are open, might even attract colorful caterpillars, which will eat the plants and then cocoon, later emerging as beautiful butterflies.

postage stamp–sized spaces using pots, boxes, and barrels. In a sectioned-off plot, plant rows of carrots, cucumbers, beans, or snap peas, which children can pick right off the vine. For larger flower or vegetable gardens, create walkways and mazes for children using straw, mulch, or flat stones, which will simultaneously add beauty to the garden and keep the soil moist (Torquati and Barber 2005).

Wildlife Gardens: From digging holes to sorting seeds, watering sprouts, recording rainfall, and charting plant growth, a wildlife garden is an ideal nature project for any early childhood outdoor setting. Welcome wildlife to your playground or garden play area by growing flowers, plants, and shrubs that attract wildlife, such as sparrows, squirrels, chipmunks, hummingbirds, robins, woodpeckers, butterflies, and an assortment of bug-munching birds. Adorn a wildlife garden with bird feeders and birdbaths. Bird feeders can be made out of almost anything, including a halved coconut shell, yogurt cup, tuna can, or plastic strawberry or tomato basket. Emily Stetson offers wonderful bird feeder and wildlife garden ideas in her book *Kids' Easy-to-Create Wildlife Habitats: For Small Spaces in City, Suburbs, or Countryside.*

Here's a quick reference chart for attracting birds and other wildlife to a class wildlife-garden project.

Nature Spark

Visit the Wildforms: Gardening for Wildlife website (www.wildforms.co.uk) for a variety of bug and animal homes that welcome little critters to an outdoor garden or play area. Whether a guest visits or not, these homes are sure to enhance the garden's decor and explorative play.

TO ATTRACT	PLANT
Hummingbirds	Trumpet vines
Dragonflies	A natural and balanced pond environment with flowers *Note*: Inform children that dragonflies do not sting or bite.
Squirrels	Pinecones, acorns, and pine seeds
Butterflies	Brightly colored flowers, such as coneflowers, zinnias, cosmos, and marigolds; buddleia (butterfly bush); flat stones for perching and basking in the sun
Robins	Berry and fruit bushes, as well as extramoist soil with fat earthworms
Ladybugs	Plants and herbs such as cilantro, dill, and cosmos

Sensory Gardens: A sensory garden is a hands-on academic bonanza. A garden full of earthworms, chocolate mint herbs, prickly roses, and lamb's ears will reap tremendous rewards. Other ideas for wonderful and contrasting sensory gardens include jasmine (peculiar scent), pussy willows (soft texture), strawflowers (dry, papery texture), and gourds (rattling sound).

Nature Spark

For areas with uncooperative weather, first plant flower or vegetable seeds inside—sunflower seeds grow quickly indoors. An excellent resource for classroom gardening is *Grow Lab: A Complete Guide to Gardening in the Classroom* from the National Gardening Association. The book provides great details on how to plan and plant an indoor flower garden.

Nature Spark

Roly-polies (pill bugs) are commonly found in compost piles, and most children find them mesmerizing. They enjoy watching roly-polies roll up and move. Let students collect several to observe for a few days. Place the bugs in a plastic tub with a layer of moist soil and a layer of dead wet leaves. Toss in fruit scraps for roly-polies to eat (Ross 2000).

Gourds take longer to grow, so plan accordingly. Plant a variety of colorful, insect-attracting flowers, including violets, roses, and honeysuckles. Mix and match herbs to challenge little noses with intense contrasting aromas. For example, plant lavender next to sage or chocolate mint near chives. Consider dwarf nasturtiums too. These plants are bright and cheerful with a pungent scent. Hang an assortment of wind chimes and wind socks. Use a variety of stepping-stone and walkway materials, such as wood chips and gravel, to add aesthetic flare to a sensory garden.

Container Gardens: Some schools, especially urban ones, lack sufficient soil for a garden project. When this is the case, container gardens are the next best option. A container flower, herb, or vegetable garden is created in wooden planter boxes, large pots, or barrels. Container gardens are easy to monitor and can be moved easily to catch sunlight. They can be placed just about anywhere, such as in classrooms or on a patio or rooftop (Starbuck and Olthof 2008). They can also be situated in small patches around a playground or in a fenced-in area. Other container garden ideas include hanging flowerpots inside and outside the classroom or placing them on a stepladder. Although not a container, chain-link fencing can be used to "contain" vines, such as cucumber, pea, or bean plants (Ross 2000). Hang flowerpots at the children's eye level so they can observe growth and chart progress. Container gardens can be produced with any type of container, such as old drawers, truck tires, or wagons, as long as drainage holes are provided.

Compost Gardens: A compost garden is perfect for studying the process of decomposition. Lots of earthen friends, such as earthworms and beetles, will emerge from a compost garden. Apple cores, banana peels, pineapple tops, and potato rinds decompose and become topsoil right before little eyes. You'll find additional composting ideas in chapter 3. A great resource for catapulting a composting project is *Compost, By Gosh!* by Michelle Eva Portman.

Weed Gardens: Grow weeds. Really! Children's gardening activities should include more than seeding, watering, raking, pruning, tying plants to stakes, cleaning tools, cutting, and harvesting.

Be sure to include the weeding aspect. With a weed garden, children will discover how, if left unattended, weeds can overtake a garden and choke out plant life. Chart, compare, and contrast what too much or too little water does to weeds.

As you pull your garden ideas and projects together, take advantage of any and all community resources. Here's a quick list to consider when collecting donations:

- Check nurseries or seed companies for seeds and plants.

- Check local hardware stores for donations or discounts on gardening tools, such as child-sized spades, trowels, fencing, watering cans, and other accessories, such as birdhouses and feeders.

- Send a newsletter home asking for materials, time, talent, or ideas.

- Contact a high school or sorority group for help with heavy work.

- Visit www.kidsgardening.com for additional tips and ideas (Starbuck and Olthof 2008).

Be sure to thank donors with a letter or photographs of children's work. A letter to the newspaper editor is also a good way to thank community donors.

Nature Spark

Introduce children to tumbleweeds. A formal definition might include "a windblown plant." Show children pictures of tumbleweeds. Have them draw one in their nature journal. Read *The Three Little Javelinas* by Susan Lowell. It's a wonderfully illustrated, Southwestern version of the three little pigs replete with tumbleweeds. It's also available in Spanish for bilingual students.

Closing Thoughts

As John Muir, a famous American naturalist, states, "When we try to pick out anything by itself, we find it hitched to everything else in the universe" (Muir 1911, 211). Bringing children closer to their natural world is possible largely because almost everything a child engages in has roots in nature. Bringing children closer to nature is also one of the most rewarding gifts we can offer in this day and age. Children become closer to nature when they interact with peers outdoors and are stimulated by new insights. They learn to respect their environment as they see it in a clearer, more detailed light. When children are brought closer to nature, they realize not only its beauty, but also their role as its future caretakers.

2

The more slowly trees
grow at first, the sounder
they are at the core.

—Henry David Thoreau

Developmentally Appropriate "Natural" Classroom Practice

Susan Isaacs asserts in her book *The Nursery Years* (1929, 10), "Through play . . . he adds to his knowledge of the world. . . . No experimental scientist has a greater thirst for new facts than an ordinary healthy active child." Nature is a living scientific laboratory for play and learning. Whether a handful of shiny rocks collected on a walk, grass-stained knees, or a gust of wind against a face, nature and children interact daily. A child's curiosity is sparked when she makes contact with nature on the playground, on a hike, or on a field trip. To bring out the nature lover in a child, integrate the natural world into everyday classroom curriculum, allowing abstract concepts to become more relevant and meaningful.

The guidelines for developmentally appropriate practice (DAP) from the National Association for the Education of Young Children (Copple and Bredekamp 2009) identify best practices in early childhood programs. The DAP guidelines provide educators with appropriate materials and activities to stimulate and challenge children in developmental areas such as physical, social, emotional, and intellectual growth, and they provide educators with a blueprint for constructing

Nature Spark

A quick DAP curriculum checklist:

❏ My classroom activities and experiences actively engage children.
❏ Play in my classroom is healthy and teacher supported.
❏ My curriculum is integrated and multifaceted.
❏ My teaching strategies cater to student progress.

(Copple and Bredekamp 2008)

best practices across the curriculum. Three principles define developmentally appropriate practice for helping children learn (Kostelnik 1993):

- Apply what you know about learning and children's development to your curriculum and teaching strategies.

- Treat children as individuals, not as a whole group.

- Show children respect—recognize their growth and be patient as they develop and learn.

Incorporating nature into the curriculum enhances it. By simply integrating a variety of themes, projects, and a diverse play menu, children will more readily grasp and make connections to other academic lessons (Tu 2006). Turn the three defining principles listed above into questions to help orient classroom lessons to nature. Ask yourself the following:

- Is this lesson or strategy in keeping with what I know about child development and learning? Is it suitable for nature learning?

- Does this lesson or strategy take into account a child's individual needs while she is outdoors?

- Does this lesson or strategy demonstrate respect for the child while he is exploring nature?

Children are born researchers and scientists. They thrive on dreams of becoming birds and butterflies rather than objectifying them (Sobel 1996). Children naturally ask questions and crave experiments through hands-on opportunities in and out of the classroom. Based on such knowledge, integrating nature-driven experiences into the classroom is not only pertinent, it can be accomplished using easier methods than you might think! If the defining principles are applied to open-ended exploration and wonderment, outcomes will prove successful.

Another question for you to ask yourself as you prepare to bring students closer to nature is this: "What do I want my students to do or to feel as a result of this nature-oriented activity, lesson, or unit?" Write your answers down. They may assist you in reorganizing classroom philosophies about the use of nature in the curriculum.

A Nature-Oriented Classroom Curriculum

A learning environment should communicate to children who they are and what they may aspire to be. A successful early-learning environment results when the teacher understands student developmental goals, interests, and characteristics. An inspiring, nature-based, hands-on curriculum supports a healthy learning environment and the development of children's social, emotional, cognitive, creative, and physical skills (Woyke 2004). Specific classroom practices—such as hands-on science experiments, logs, and journals—have creative and thought-provoking questions, as well as an assortment of play projects and continual open-ended problem solving that develop a child's inner naturalistic intelligence and thirst for nature (Bellanca, Chapman, and Swartz 1997). To steer your classroom setting to such nature-oriented play practices, review the following questions (Curtis and Carter 2005):

- What message does my classroom environment give children about how to interact with and treat nature?

- Does my classroom have flexible areas that can be used for open-ended and single-purpose nature activities?

- Are there nature-driven places in my classroom where children can go to get away, relax, or daydream? Can they work without interruption?

- Are novel nature items, such as interesting shells, rocks, and crystals, used to further spark a child's interest in nature?

What follows are several ideas for transforming your classroom into one that nurtures a nature-driven atmosphere:

Manipulative Play: A curious child at a table filled with open-ended materials is a powerful learning combination. Children use their senses and diverse materials to explore and extend learning. Incorporate an open-ended manipulative table with puzzles, games, and natural items, such as pebbles, pieces of bark, twigs, and leaves. Encourage students to re-create scenes or objects of nature with manipulatives. This will

Nature Spark

As you construct nature stations for students, implement as many of the following components as possible:

- Use realistic nature pictures, symbols, and words to communicate with children.
- Use direct eye contact and elaborate gestures to express key points and objectives.
- Explain station directions as a group as well as one-on-one to students who may require more individual instruction.

Nature Spark

Explore lending libraries for borrowing or purchasing classroom materials. Be sure to provide children with many options that encourage interesting tactile opportunities, as well as music and movement. Centers should allow children to use all their sensory modalities—visual, auditory, and kinesthetic. Keep an eye open for high-interest activities to which children flock (Watson and McCathren 2009). Be sure all children have a chance to engage in favorite play areas.

support abstract concept learning. In addition to natural specimens, provide construction paper, natural clay, papier-mâché, Styrofoam, and pipe cleaners (Danoff-Burg 2002). Organize toys and materials clearly. Teach students to keep items in bins and off the floor, as well as to push chairs in when finished playing. Carry over this concept to all center-time play—indoors or out.

Sensory Play: A nature-oriented sensory-play area is a highly effective learning tool when led by student interests. Sensory play provides wonderful opportunities for nature-oriented exploration and discovery. Although sand and water are starting points for captivating sensory play, adding dirt with worms or soggy fall leaves catapults a child's wonderment. Toss in several safe tools amid squishy nature materials. Measuring cups, funnels, egg beaters, garlic presses, magnifying glasses, and tongs are great options. Listed below are additional possibilities to fill a sensory-play table:

- small vinyl or plastic animals, such as bendable animals, pom-pom animals, expanding zoo animals and floating animals (perfect for a sensory water table), floppy animals, farm animals, and sea animals; visit Rhode Island Novelty at www.rinovelty.com

- dandelion puffs (consider student allergies)

- crushed cherry blossoms and flower petals

- frozen gelatin cubes (good sensory experience as children explore texture and color)

- seeds and acorns

- snow and icicles brought in from outdoors and mixed with ice chips

- wildflowers and pinecones

- authentic seashells, aquarium gravel, pebbles, and stones in lots of colors

- buttons, beads, birdseed, and beans

- cornmeal, oatmeal, confetti, and crayon shavings

- dirt (soft clods or mud)

- fabric scraps

- flour or powdered milk

- pasta and noodles (try Art-A-Roni)

Nature Spark

A sensory play area can become a patchwork quilt. Include burlap bits, carpet chunks, corduroy, cotton balls, denim, fur, gauze, netting, silk, terrycloth, velvet, vinyl, and wool. Mix fabrics with sand or dry dirt.

- popcorn (popped or kernels)

- rice (try buckets of colored rice, www.eNasco.com /earlylearning)

- sand (colored or natural; wet or dry)

- shaving cream, sawdust, and shredded paper

- sponges (various shapes and sizes; wet or dry)

- water tinted with food coloring, food extracts, Silly String, ice cubes, or other toss-ins

Add cups, containers, and funnels to a sensory table and let the students follow their interests as they navigate the table's contents.

Scientific Play: Classroom science play gives children the opportunity to experiment, explore, and practice scientific skills such as classifying, comparing, observing, and predicting. A scientific play area is best situated in a sunny area of the classroom with a low table displaying materials children can freely investigate, such as rocks, plants, and gadgets. Refer to the adjacent Nature Spark for additional creative materials. Simple items, such as a mortar and pestle or a rolling pin and cutting board, are terrific for generating science play. A science play area should include open-ended materials that are regularly rotated and made accessible to all children. Scientific play areas should also include means for recording data, such as writing and art materials; plain, graph, and tracing paper; calendars; and measurement tools (Hachey and Butler 2009).

Small critters—such as insects, snails, hermit crabs, earthworms, and ants—are great for scientific observation. Some ideas include the following:

- Millipedes: These multilegged critters are sometimes confused with centipedes. At a science table, have students graph and draw the differences in their nature journal. Centipedes have stingers. Millipedes don't. Millipedes have twice as many legs as centipedes. Millipedes have round bodies. Centipedes have flat bodies.

- Grasshoppers: At a classroom science table, have children set up an "exploratorium" for grasshoppers, crickets, and ladybugs. Students can observe these creatures in a small terrarium full of soil, leaves, and lettuce. Ladybugs eat

Nature Spark

Stock up on the following nature specimens for learning centers and hands-on science experiments:

- abandoned beehives
- abandoned birds' nests
- bark
- clean, dry eggshells
- dried flowers
- fall leaves
- feathers
- fossils
- gourds
- "helicopter" maple seeds
- insects
- milkweed pods
- pinecones
- potting soil
- rocks and gravel
- seashells
- seeds

Nature Spark

Lead children on a short butterfly walk around the playground. As you walk, have each child hold the shoulders of the person in front of him. Point out to the group that they have lots of legs—just like a caterpillar. Right before the end of the walk, ask students to release one another's shoulders and fly away like butterflies. Use the walk as an extension activity for studying the butterfly cycle.

Nature Spark

Tarantulas are wonderful seasonal pets, especially during their molting process. Tarantulas eat crickets and other small insects, which children enjoy bringing from home. Crickets can be purchased at pet shops as well.

aphids found on outdoor plants. Have students release ladybugs after a few hours of observation; they are environmentally friendly insects.

- Butterflies: The life cycle of a butterfly can be displayed creatively at a science table. Visit www.insectlore.com for ideas. Students will marvel as they observe wooly caterpillars inching along plant stems. Have students draw and write about the butterfly life cycle in their nature journals. Refer to the sample butterfly life-cycle illustration below.

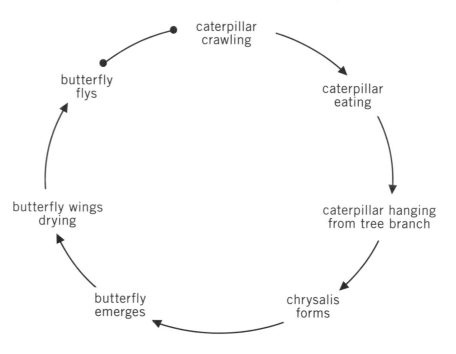

THE BUTTERFLY CYCLE

Classroom Pets: Caring for a class pet can give children the chance to study nature and to develop critical-thinking skills. When children have opportunities to responsibly care for animals daily, they "practice nurturing behaviors that help them interact in kind and gentle ways" (Rosenow 2008, 10). Have students take turns feeding the class pet and discuss how it needs food and water just as they do. If the pet dies, let the class decide what they should do rather than hide its death from them. When selecting a class pet, safety, simplicity, and creativity should remain at the forefront. The class critter should also harness student interest. Several classroom pet suggestions include the following:

- African land crabs
- newts
- tarantulas
- turtles (land or water)
- hamsters
- guinea pigs
- gerbils
- rabbits
- parrots or parakeets
- exotic or tropical fish

Music Play: At a musical play area, children can listen to music, sing along, and play instruments such as gourds, rain sticks, and dried honey-locust pods that have been turned into rhythm shakers. Encourage children to create and perform musical dances to rhythm instruments. A nature-driven music area might offer CDs that feature the sounds of water, wind, a thunderstorm, a rain forest, ocean waves, spring frogs, or chirping crickets. Allow students to use headphones to enjoy a variety of music, including classical pieces with an emphasis on nature, such as Beethoven's Sixth Symphony, African drumming, Indian *bhamgra* music, Irish and Scottish jigs, and salsa. Let students make natural musical instruments out of seeds, pods, and shells (Woyke 2004).

Natural Art: Natural elements have high play value, and open-ended nature materials have wonderful potential in artistic creations. Smooth or coarse cobblestones become canvases on which children paint; twigs and sticks become artistic patterns in collages or rubbings. Natural materials are free, and children can search for them on hikes. At a natural-art play area, incorporate a variety of media, such as chalk, charcoal, crayons, markers, and colored pencils. Place paper on easels, tables, and walls, and of course make it available outside as well.

A natural-art play area can help children extend cognitive thinking skills from simple to more complex. Try the following ideas:

Nature Spark

Encourage students to express themselves and their interests while painting to musical selections. Make music available while at a music play area. Many types of nature-oriented music work well indoors and out. Possibilities include the following:

- *Bolero* by Maurice Ravel
- *Carnival of the Animals* by Camille Saint-Saëns
- "May There Always Be Sunshine" by Lev Oshanin
- *Peter and the Wolf* by Sergei Prokofiev
- "Pines of Rome" by Ottorino Respighi
- "Sunrise" from Ferde Grofé's *Grand Canyon Suite*
- "The William Tell Overture" by Gioachino Rossini

- Have children draw pictures of obvious nature changes—such as weather or the seasons—rather than write about them. Children can explain their drawing to the class.

- Share artwork from various cultures and countries. Spotlight well-known artists such as Claude Monet, Vincent van Gogh, Faith Ringgold, and Georgia O'Keeffe. As students explore the paintings, they will gain inspiration for their artistic work. Share other art, such as Gee's Bend quilts, Inuit carvings, and African or Asian masks.

- Encourage children to sign their artwork. Share examples of artists' signatures on paintings.

Dramatic Play: Young children need time to daydream and become things. Transform dramatic play centers into stimulating, nature-oriented areas, such as veterinarian clinics, dark caves with denning bears, fall vegetable stands, or summer campgrounds. Children can make masks and become jungle animals while moving to creative music. Discuss and reenact the bee "waggle dance." Bees use the waggle dance to communicate with other bees about the location and quality of food (Danoff-Burg 2002). Costumes and props are limitless for waggle-dance dramatic play. Encourage children to further research the waggle dance online. *The Magic School Bus Inside a Beehive* by Joanna Cole and Bruce Degen is an excellent book for introducing bee behavior.

Language and Literacy Play: Language and early literacy development is greatly enhanced with a print-rich environment. Incorporate a relaxing area for children to lounge and read nature magazines, such as *Your Big Backyard* or *Ranger Rick* (from the National Wildlife Federation), class-made nature books, colorful maps, and flower or plant catalogs. Display beautifully illustrated children's books that foster a love for nature, such as *A Tree Is Nice* by Janice May Udry, *The Salamander Room* by Anne Mazer, and almost anything by Eric Carle. Set up comfy pillows, chairs, and comforters nearby. Encourage story sharing among students. Make boxes of nature items available, such as animal puppets, animal-character flannel boards, and CDs with nature stories and songs.

Weather Charting Play Station: Children are naturally curious about the weather. Observing and feeling heat, wind, rain, and snow

Nature Spark

For butterfly or bird play, try the following idea. Gather several large refrigerator boxes, cut them into sheets, and have children lie down on top of them on their backs with their arms outstretched. Starting at the neck, trace around the children, but instead of following along the underside of the arm, draw a straight line from the wrist to the waist, then down on both sides to the knees. Now have children cut out the wings and decorate them. Use heavy twine to tie wings onto students' arms (Sobel 1996). Extend the activity and make child-sized nests from plastic wading pools filled with sheets.

will do the job right! Some questions are inevitable: "How big is the sky?" "Why do worms come out after it rains?" Have children chart daily weather patterns on a large piece of graph paper and then use a dictating machine and take turns as the weather announcer. Use circle time to share and discuss observations.

Computer and Technology Play Station: Include an area offering technology with developmentally appropriate nature software. The appendix lists several suggestions. As you ponder software selections, ask what about the subject appeals to students. Try to recall what it was about the subject that appealed to *you* as a child. Today the possibilities are endless with creative nature-oriented software. Use videos, websites, and audiobooks as well as computer software to instruct.

Playful Window Watching: Changing seasonal weather is perfect for window watching. Set up a classroom area near a window where children can observe hanging bird feeders, birdbaths, gardens, or a tree full of nesting birds. Set up furniture, such as stools and stepladders. Other window-watching ideas include the following:

- Make and display a dust bath by a classroom window. Dig a shallow area in the dirt and crumble dirt so birds can bathe in it.

- Turn a simple garbage-can lid into a birdbath. Make sure it is always full of water for birds to drink.

- Let children observe clouds from the window. Have them draw diagrams of what they see in their nature journals.

Nature Spark

Many children with special needs benefit from the use of computerized learning centers. Ask for recommendations from an expert before choosing software that supports children with special needs (Watson and McCathren 2009).

Incorporate Hands-On Learning Centers

Time outdoors is important for young children. It allows them the freedom to explore, choose their own activities, and use their imagination without teacher distraction. Nature can be brought inside and turned into fascinating and effective classroom learning centers. Learning centers as described here differ from free-play nature stations because they are directed by specific objectives. An ideal example might include a hands-on bird center. When leaves have fallen from trees in late fall and early winter, it is easy to see deserted birds' or wasps' nests. After collecting several empty nests, have students carefully pull one apart to see what is inside. Have students look closely at how the nest was made. Discuss with students how nests can be either finely intertwined or loosely made and how they can be found in a variety of sizes. The possibilities for hands-on, nature-oriented learning centers are endless.

Food Center: Fresh food products promote natural exploration. Whether cooking or investigating food, the use of sensory skills is involved. Bring cultural diversity into a classroom food center. Whip up an array of yummy flavors and smells. Cook the following from scratch: gingerbread people, tortillas, wontons, waffles, fry bread, stir-fry, challah, hoecakes, bagels, pasta, hush puppies, latkes, and bread. Connect recipes to storybooks, nursery rhymes, and folktales. Get creative! Make "Peter, Peter Pumpkin Eater" bread or "holy moly" guacamole! Prepare and taste creations as a class. Gather permission from parents first, of course, and remember to be sensitive to children's individual food allergies.

To make cooking in the classroom manageable, keep it simple. Use simple recipes with easy directions and few ingredients. For effective and convenient cooking, it is a good idea to have a stove and mini refrigerator accessible. Perishables, such as milk and eggs, can be stored in the refrigerator. Incorporate literacy into a food center by encouraging students to draw, write, or share foods that their families commonly enjoy. Compare food sketches with classmates.

Sorting Center: Learning centers based on children's eagerness to explore the natural world can provide many learning opportunities. A sorting center is ideal because it enhances curiosity and scientific skills, such as observing, comparing, organizing, and classifying. At a sorting center, children can construct patterns using size, measurement, shape, and position. Sorting objects are abundant and include the following:

- Leaves of any variety

- Seeds such as sunflower, pumpkin, chestnut, beans, and sesame

- Sink and float objects, such as marbles, pine needles, and wadded aluminum foil (Moomaw and Hieronymus 1997)

Nature Spark

For a refreshing outdoor treat on warm spring days, mix diced jicama with diced seedless watermelon and lime juice. Sprinkle with fresh cilantro, sesame seeds, and alfalfa sprouts. Ask questions such as "What is this?" and discuss how and where the ingredients of this Mexican snack are grown. Visit www .fruitsandveggiesmatter.gov for additional flavorful, multi-cultural snacks.

Nature Spark

An enclosed fire pit can serve as a fascinating gathering place. Children can sit or stand around it and share diverse food and story experiences. Outdoor cooking is a part of many cultures, and it is a wonderful way to connect children to nature. With close supervision, children can roast food with long sticks or bake in aluminum foil (Sutterby and Frost 2002).

Plant Center: Displaying a variety of plants in the classroom for children to water and prune is a simple yet fantastic way to ignite natural exploration in the classroom. Children will enjoy observing simple plants, from roots and growing processes to life-cycles and species categorization. Gardening tools are not necessary for sprouting simple seeds at a plant center. Children can use their hands. Combine an insect unit with a plant center. Make a collection of caterpillars, ants, or flies; house the insects in clear plastic deli containers. Steer budding scientists and naturalists to additional classroom resources that nurture insect and plant interests. *Peterson First Guide to Insects of North America* is a wonderful option (Danoff-Burg 2002).

Water Center: A basic water table can reinforce numerous mathematical and science skills while nurturing productive nature-oriented play. A water table can froth with bubbles or be thickened with cornstarch. A water table can be colored or scented with extracts. A successful water table can teach concepts of empty/full, thick/thin, shallow/deep, greater than/less than, heavy/light, before/after, and others. The appendix offers additional resources for water play.

Soil Center: A soil center is versatile and should always contain high-quality soil (avoid soil filled with unsafe debris). The objective of a soil center is for children to explore and experience a variety of earthy elements. Natural clay, dirt, mud, and sand can be used. Provide a variety of tools for children to use. Here is one possible lesson. Have students pour an inch of soil into a pie pan. Using a cookie cutter as a guide, let children outline their design with small nature manipulatives, such as pebbles or small twigs. Help students sprinkle seeds inside their design. Let students use a spray bottle to water the seeds. Loosely cover the pie pan with plastic wrap and place in sunlight. Children will soon see the soil's power when mixed with seeds, water, and sunlight. Have students perform the experiment with other soils, such as clay and sand. Did the seeds sprout? Log outcomes.

Chick-Hatching Center: Bring in an incubator containing several chicken eggs. Set up a special egg-hatching countdown calendar. Have children monitor and observe changes in chicken egg size, shape, and color. As the eggs hatch, have children

Nature Spark

To display seeds, nuts, and other natural items, use a cupcake stand. They are inexpensive and available with three tiers. Save used vitamin bottles for sorting and storing items. Simply soak bottles in warm water to remove labels.

Nature Spark

Beans are simple plants for children to grow. They can be planted outdoors in hills or rows or on poles. Bean seeds are big and easy for children to handle. Display and discuss different bean varieties, such as green beans, yellow beans, lima beans (butter beans), navy beans, black-eyed peas (cow peas), and soybeans.

focus on how the chicks work their way out of the eggshells. Have students draw responses to observations in their nature journals. Extend the chick-hatching center with additional activities after the chicks hatch. Discuss what baby chicks eat and reasons why they require continual warmth. Culminate the chicks' release to a farm with a field trip to their new home.

Field Trips, Nature Hikes, and Outdoor Obstacle Courses

Learning is more meaningful when children are allowed the freedom to be inquisitive, adventurous, innovative, loud, and messy (White 2008). When field trips, hikes, or obstacle courses can be arranged, they are wonderful outdoor activities for children. The richness of nature makes these activities meaningful. They are a great way to give children concrete experiences that enhance their learning outside the classroom. Children build on and create new ideas about their play as they interact and experience nature in as many contexts as possible and by using all their senses. Before outings, have a discussion during circle time. Ask open-ended questions before the trip to stimulate thinking. After the adventure, have students draw experiences in their nature journals. If you have enough parent volunteers, break students into small groups for more individual interaction. If possible, preview trips, hikes, and obstacle courses to better prepare for student questions.

Field Trips

Field trips are an important part of any early childhood curriculum and must have a purpose to have meaning to children. Field trips are extensions of what is taking place in the classroom and should be kept simple so they are manageable and developmentally appropriate for young children. Many things need to be considered when planning an effective field trip: How long will the trip take? How will children's safety, ages, attention spans, special needs, and interest levels be considered? How much adult supervision is required?

Field trips should include postvisit activities. Consider the following:

- Have children make scrapbooks or do a nature-based project related to their adventure. Encourage pasting of natural specimens collected on the field trip.

- Host a family recipe night after a trip to an apple orchard or cornfield. Encourage families to bring in their yummiest recipes to taste and exchange.

- Make a mural. Have students draw their favorite part of the trip.

- Have children write thank-you letters to the organization that hosted the trip.

- Plan an off-season visit. Compare trip differences.

On field trips children can become ornithologists, geologists, and archaeologists. The sky's the limit! Consider the following ideas.

Museums: From art to natural history, museums cover many topics for exploration as well as exciting hands-on exhibits. Museums offer chances to nurture individual curiosities. Prepare children for museum trips by planning pre- and postvisit activities, which will cement newfound knowledge and interests. Refer to chapter 4 for a list of questions to use to prepare students for museum trips. The questions are also suitable for other field trips.

Lumber Mills: A field trip to a lumber mill will grant children first-hand access to technology. Modern mills require hard hats and earplugs for children to safely observe how different trees—such as maple, beech, and oak—are turned into boards, chips, and sawdust. Children will marvel at the machinery, although noisy, as well as the feel and smell of fresh sawdust, stripped bark, and log rings. A lumber-mill field trip will require several chaperones.

Farms: Farm life can present interesting hands-on horticultural knowledge and sensory activities. Farm life confronts children with everyday life experiences that are often unfamiliar to them, such as milking cows or feeding chickens. Barnyard animals, such as pigs, horses, ducks, chickens, hens, and roosters, require different care, which will generate endless

Nature Spark

Playing in a fresh-tilled field—especially in stocking feet—is a fantastic sensory experience for children. If possible, allow students to watch the farmer till the field. Explain the need for the field soil to be turned over and nurtured.

exploration and questions for young children. A field trip to a farm might also provide opportunities to pick fresh veggies and push wheelbarrows.

Patches: Children have an affinity for pumpkin and berry patches. Regardless of patch location or type, the experience will cultivate a child's sense of wonder. Patches have individual growing, pollinating, and picking procedures to discuss with children. Field trips to pumpkin and berry patches offer hayrides, petting corrals, and corn pits as well as opportunities to pick fresh produce. Pumpkin and berry patches make wonderful fall field trips.

Orchards and Vineyards: A field trip to an apple orchard can be an enchanting firsthand opportunity for children to see how apples are grown and distributed to grocery stores. When children visit an apple orchard or a vineyard, they will have a level of sensory experience and tactile freedom not found in a classroom. Select fresh apples for making homemade apple juice and applesauce as a post-field-trip activity. Visit during the fall and then again in the spring so children can appreciate the growing process. Prepare students for an orchard field trip. Set up a center with an apple-seed sorting activity or a plate of different apple varieties for students to taste.

Cornfields: Touring a granary where corn is stored will send the sparks of a child's natural curiosity flying. On a field trip to a cornfield, children will be able to study corn and its silk. Have students trek through a corn maze. Interview the farmers who tend the cornfields. Compare Indian corn to sweet corn. The possibilities are endless!

Greenhouses: The surprises of a blooming plant can instantly capture a child's attention and desire to investigate. Visiting a greenhouse will allow students to experience plants in different stages, sizes, and conditions. If possible, visit several times to view and document the growth of seedlings. Have students transplant their work into a class garden. Maize and sunflower seeds are easy to transplant; both transform from tiny seeds to towering plants with minimal student care. Another plant that will allow children to witness a plant's whole life cycle in a short amount of time is lettuce. Lettuce grows phenomenally fast. Its entire plant cycle unwinds in a few weeks.

Honey Farms: A trip to a honey farm is full of valuable lessons. With students, discuss pollination, the importance of bees on a farm, bee behavior, and how bees make and gather honey. Reading *The Berenstain Bears' Class Trip* by Jan and Mike Berenstain to students is a simple pretrip activity that students will enjoy. Brother Bear's class is going on a trip to a honey farm. Mama and Papa are class helpers on the trip. Follow up the story with a connected writing or drawing activity in nature journals.

Pet Shops: A trip to a local pet shop to view aquariums full of frogs, snakes, lizards, newts, and an assortment of fish is a simple field trip for youngsters. The children will perceive the adventure as a mini zoo complete with turtles, rabbits, chameleons, and more. Simple children's nature programs available on PBS, TLC, or the Discovery Channel are wonderful connecting options before venturing to a pet shop. Follow up the field trip by allowing children to bring in their pets. Have a class pet parade, and invite other classrooms.

Nature Hikes

Nature hikes can lead children toward wonderful sensory challenges, such as trekking through lush grass, balancing on fallen logs, or feeling the hot sun against their faces. When activities engage children in novel ways, they learn to focus and better express their ideas. Promote the development of sensory awareness and an assortment of other skills through nature hikes. Take time to discuss and evaluate with students what they are experiencing as they hike. Let students use a digital camera and place the photos in their nature journals. Give children individual "goodie" bags, so as they hike along a path they can search and collect many different nature specimens to sort and label at a later time. Possible nature-hike ideas include the following:

Theme Hike: On a theme hike have children focus on a particular theme, such as nature colors, shadows, seeds, insects, signs of the season, or types of trees or birds. Connect theme hikes to art projects. After a "color" hike, have students mix paint to match the colors they recall having observed. Have them paint objects with these distinct colors.

Nature Spark

Field trips to a shoreline or outdoor amphitheater are not out of the question for young children. Both require lots of supervision but would be wonderful places for students to collect nature specimens and data and then discuss observations. What about a visit to a community rose garden?

Nature Spark

While on sensory hikes, let children look for acorns, fallen bark chunks, pinecones and pine needles, and leaves of all shapes and sizes. Have children run their fingers over the top of a tree stump or feel cold mud. Bring magnifying glasses, binoculars, sunglasses, kaleidoscopes, butterfly nets, and prisms to enhance a sensory hike. Encourage children to listen for sounds, such as a bird chirping, the wind whooshing, a dog barking, or dry leaves crunching as you walk in them. When you return to class, use collected items to make a nature mobile with yarn and a hanger. A nature collage is another resourceful idea for items collected on a hike.

Nature Spark

Pita bread that is halved and filled with sliced ham, cheese, and an assortment of veggies makes a great hiking snack for children.

Alphabet Hike: Divide students into teams, each with a captain. Any player from either team who sees something beginning with the letter *A* and pertaining to nature names it. The captain writes down the word. Members from that team then look for something beginning with *B*. The team that gets the furthest through the alphabet before the hike ends wins!

Sensory Hike: While hiking, focus children's attention on what they hear or feel. For example, ask, "Do you hear birds chirping? Wind whistling? Woodpeckers pecking? Crickets chirping?" Even locusts make notable noises. Have children feel bark, leaves, grass, and rocks. If possible, purposely have students trudge through thick mud or wade in a cool river to catch crawdads, minnows, or tadpoles that will captivate their senses and heighten their sensory awareness. Children will enjoy gathering flower heads, such as dandelions. Discuss and examine the sensory differences between dandelion heads and dandelion seed puffs.

Search Hike: While on a search hike, have children focus on discovering wildlife in the air, on the ground, or in a stream. Search for nests, animal tracks, droppings, tree holes, burrows, and other signs of life. Students can draw discoveries in their nature journals or compare them on large chart paper. Take a pocket-sized *Golden Guide* along. Use it to look up questions children might have about discovered items or unknown flowers and plants.

Cleanup Hike: Organize a hike to clean up surrounding natural environments, such as a local park, nature trail, or school playground. Take along trash bags and nonlatex gloves for each child. Connect recycling projects to a cleanup hike.

"I Spy" Hike: Children gain knowledge and create theories about nature when they use observational skills to answer questions about how things within it work. Use an "I Spy" hike to focus on the small details of nature. Have students examine a spiderweb or a dandelion poking its head through a sidewalk crack. Have students spy something beginning with the letter *B*. Use a puppet prop, such as Bertha Beetle, to enforce the connection between nature and literacy.

Plant Hike: While hiking, have children try to find as many different plants as possible. Be sure to address any toxic plants they might encounter. Students can use their senses on a plant hike to learn more about the plant world. Have children smell various flowers or pinch a leaf, stem, or root and smell it. Feel the texture of bark and leaves. Lie on the ground and look up at the tree to see the patterns in its branches and leaves.

Color-Match Hike: Gather a variety of paint chips from a local paint store. Have students match paint samples to natural outdoor colors while hiking. Draw and write connections in nature journals.

Bird-Watching Hike: While on a bird-watching hike, have children observe and draw birds. Look for nesting birds in eaves and trees or on utility lines. Introduce words such as *migration*, *plumage*, and *perch* for nature journals or word walls. Discuss the basic parts of a bird and have students label its parts. Students will benefit from learning to use proper terminology when describing birds. Refer to the following illustration. Discuss local species. Have students listen for birds chirping;

Nature Spark

Encourage students to use as many adjectives as possible when describing what they see on nature walks, whether verbally or in a nature journal. For example, a child may express, "Mrs. Cross, I saw a spider!" You could prompt a lengthier response: "Wow, TJ! Did it look like the eight-legged hairy spider we saw last week on the playground?"

Nature Spark

Children will enjoy observing and learning about birds in their area, as well as learning the secrets of turning their school yard into a home for wild birds. Visit www.a-home-for-wild-birds.com for wonderful information on bird watching. Make and hang milk-jug bird feeders, suet feeders, and platform and soda-bottle bird feeders. Discuss the state bird with students or why it is that female birds often do not sing while male birds have beautiful voices. In their nature journals, have students section off a few pages to paste pictures of local birds.

Invite further exploration on hikes by asking questions. For example, a bird-watching hike might spark questions, such as "What does this particular bird eat?" "What color are its eggs?" "What nesting materials does the bird use?" "What are the differences between a female and male bird?" Use a Venn diagram for comparison purposes.

pigeons are common in urban areas. As a creative twist, have students walk and bob their heads and flap their wings (arms) like a pigeon as a prehike focusing activity.

Seed-Discovery Hike: A seed-discovery hike can be easily implemented in the autumn months when plants, weeds, and trees are shedding. Have students look for seeds in a variety of sizes, shapes, colors, and textures. Discuss with students how seeds need water, warmth, food, and air to sprout. With an abundance of seeds, students can make collages and seed shakers for the music area, as well as add seeds to their fingerpaint.

Fragrance Hike: Take children on a fragrance hike around the school playground or neighborhood and see how many smells of the season they can identify. A few possibilities include the smell of wet soil, the smell of fresh air after a rain shower, or the smell of flowers.

Outdoor Obstacle Courses

Young children require playtime outdoors. As Jan White (2008, 1) confirms, children's "minds and bodies develop best when they have free access to stimulating outdoor environments." An outdoor obstacle course is a hands-on experience where children of all ages will be challenged developmentally in multisensory and multifaceted ways. Obstacle courses encourage children to work cooperatively with peers, develop spatial awareness, enhance gross-motor skills, and engage in social situations that improve their ability to negotiate (Griffin and Rinn 1998). A key ingredient to making any obstacle course successful is to get children involved in producing it. Obstacle courses should be slightly more advanced than children's developmental level (Griffin and Rinn 1998). Observation during the building process will quickly make you aware if the course is too easy, too hard, or just right! Close and proper supervision, as well as safety, should remain at the forefront of obstacle-course building. Additional goals of an outdoor obstacle course include the following:

- provide outdoor experiences for creative social play

- promote physical activity

- encourage exploration and adventure
- encourage problem solving

OBSTACLE COURSE EQUIPMENT

Obstacle course equipment is only limited by space and imagination. Listed below are suggestions to get the process started and creative juices flowing.

- **Discarded tires** are available at most automotive stores. Tires can be used for a variety of purposes on an obstacle course, including stepping mazes and as weights to hold other course items—a mat, for example—securely. Construct a tire trail for an obstacle course. Systematically lay out three to five tires, each filled with a variety of play options and sensory stuff. For example, soupy sand and linking toys at tire 1. Fill tire 2 with wooden blocks. Place an assortment of cars and dump trucks in tire 3. Offer a variety of play experiences at each tire. Old tractor tires can also be turned into stimulating play equipment. Paint tires for flare.

  When using tires in children's play, it is important to position the tires so they don't accumulate rainwater; standing water can be a source of mosquito breeding. It is also important to be aware that rubber tires contain volatile organic compounds (VOCs) and may also contain heavy metals. To prevent exposure to these hazards, be sure tires are not torn or crumbling. Always clean tires and check them for glass and nails. Drill holes in them to release rainwater.

- Bury an **old boat or canoe** in the ground as a creative obstacle-course station. Add creative accessories, such as play fishing poles, nets, and tackle boxes full of rubber worms and sensory sorts. Mount a wheel from an old stroller (preferably a large all-terrain wheel) as a steering wheel for a pirate adventure. Do not forget the telescope and a "walking" plank!

- Most grocery stores will donate **plastic milk or bread crates** if given advance notice. The crates must be strong, so decorative crates found at department stores are not recommended for obstacle courses. Milk crates can be used to store loose play parts and materials or can be stacked as dividing walls.

Nature Spark

On days with inclement weather, set up a simple obstacle course indoors using chairs, tables with blankets over them, pillows, and carpet squares. Demonstrate a run-through of the indoor course. Encourage students to cheer each other on as they individually complete the indoor obstacle course.

Visit www.eNasco.com
/earlylearning for additional
large-motor physical gear
similar to hula hoops. For
example, you might find jump
sets and ankle-ball hops. Both
provide a fast and challenging
aerobic activity that can help
children develop upper- and
lower-body strength.

Nature Spark

Create a small outdoor
obstacle course using sturdy
boxes, such as photocopy
paper boxes, and washtubs.
Old washtubs are hefty and
can sit on the ground or
be partially buried below
the ground. Decorate each
container boldly and fill
with sand, dirt, water, small
aquarium pebbles, crunchy
fall leaves, cotton balls,
feathers, or squishy toy bugs.
Situate the containers in a
circle or square. Have children walk in and out of the
containers barefoot, in socks,
or in galoshes. Add music.

- **Cable spools** come in a variety of sizes. Ask cable television companies for donations. Some cable spools have cardboard centers, which are not recommended because their structure is too weak. Cable spools for obstacle courses need to be sturdy and able to withstand the weather and the weight of children. Cable spools can be used as seats, stages, or art tables.

- Give **hula hoops** a try! As children use their bodies to explore the hula hoops—whether stepping or jumping in and out of them or tossing them into the air—they develop spatial awareness (Odoy and Foster 1997). Situate an assortment of colored hoops in patterns on the ground. Make sure to alternate direction. Have children hop on one foot or wave their hands in the air. Instruct them to jump through the hoops pretending to be big kangaroos or small bunnies. Get creative. On an outdoor obstacle course, use hula hoops in the same way you use tires: have children step through hula hoops or hang them from a tree with sturdy rope and toss balls back and forth. Hula hoops can be used to hang sound items, such as metal teakettles that children can clang. Duct tape or shower rings will secure items from hanging hula hoops. Children can also hula with hoops in the traditional manner or roll them round and round.

- Most appliance stores are happy to donate **big boxes** for classrooms. Children can paint right on refrigerator, washer, and dryer boxes. Teachers can cut windows and doors. Be creative with cutting. Why make a boring rectangular door when you can cut an arched one? Instead of square windows, cut them in the shapes of clouds! Children respond and relate to eccentricity. Appliance boxes can also be converted into dens, tunnels, or mazes. Use paper tubes as periscopes or telescopes. Children can take turns sitting in boxes as others push them along. (Be sure to stick duct tape over any staples that may be present.) Appliance boxes can be cut down into sheets and used as stage flooring or as dramatic-play costumes.

- Use **plastic trash cans and barrels** as tunnels. Cut out their bottoms and connect them end to end. With plastic trash cans or barrels, play bucket ball with sponge balls or large bean bags. Turn several plastic trash cans upside down and throw a slab of carpet over the top to make a cave, wolf's den, submarine, or even a beehive. Children can also roll around on a playground in clean plastic barrels.

- Yes . . . **gutters**! Plastic guttering or piping can be purchased inexpensively at building supply and lumber stores, where they are normally sold to attach to roofs as rain gutters. Gutters are ideal because they are lightweight and smooth, and their curved surfaces make them safe for children. Gutters can be attached—vertically and horizontally—at the midpoint of an outside wall. Children can pour sand and water down the pipe. Children will also enjoy rolling Ping-Pong balls, marbles, or pea gravel through them. Add pitchers, pots, buckets, and stepladders to the gutter play station. Using gutters, children can see wonderful science at work!

- Use **carpet squares** as stepping-stones or flooring for outdoor play. Large pieces of carpet can create an outdoor stage for puppets and dramatic-play items. Carpet squares make perfect outdoor seats for storytelling and sharing play items under big oak trees. Make a trail of thin tree-trunk slices and carpet remnants arranged in a creative pattern. Have students walk on the trail in socks for a rich sensory experience.

- **Hop balls and potato sacks**—the originals! Lay big, bouncing hop balls and potato sacks out along an obstacle course. Fantastic for increasing body strength and balance, children don't even know they are getting a healthy workout when they use them. Have races on the playground.

- **Wedges and mats**—staples for outdoor tumbling! Use them to cushion the outer areas of obstacle courses. Mats can be turned into ramps, inclines, trails, or flooring. Wedges make great siding for play areas or freeways for "vrooming" small vehicles when situated in the dirt or sand. They are easy to clean—have children hose them down after use.

- **Plastic swimming pools**—a wonderful sensory pit for the whole body! Fill old plastic swimming pools with a variety of sensory balls, carpet squares, small pillows, and Styrofoam packing pieces. Additional items to fill a sensory pool include the following:

  - colored craft cotton balls
  - craft feathers

- popcorn kernels and beans

- rice

- small, slimy-feeling balls

- small tactile toys

- squishy, squashy sponges

- Styrofoam packing peanuts

- textured bumpy balls

- tiny nub balls

- **Wood planks and balance beams** are perfect for tightrope activities or for ramps and inclines. Children can move creatively from one activity to the next on wood planks and balance beams. Sloppy wet sand combined with wood planks, flat rocks, and log rings could ignite an instant brick-laying station on an obstacle course.

- I have yet to meet a child who does not enjoy jumping on a **mini trampoline**. This obstacle station is simple, yet promotes the most physical play. Set up a box of musical instruments for children to shake and rattle while jumping.

- Large **carpet tubes** can be acquired from carpet stores, sawed into sections, and turned into an awesome obstacle course for children to "putt-putt" balls through. A putt-putt course is wonderful for honing fine-motor skills. Use a variety of balls for putt-putt play. Children always enjoy choices.

- Craft a trail of **fall leaves** for children to run through. Rustling leaves are not only pleasurable to feel, but also amazing to hear. Dampen the leaves for a more physical activity. (Dry leaves are not as heavy as wet leaves.)

- **Textured stepping-stones** make outstanding sensory obstacle courses for children! Hobby stores offer flat stones that can easily be turned into pathways. Sturdy metal pie pans or old Frisbees make great pathway stones. Use a variety of other textures to create a sensory pathway. Try bricks, bread crates, wood chips, linoleum squares, large tiles, mulch, gravel, sod patches, or flagstones. Secure stepping-stones to prevent sliding. Tunnels or age-appropriate ramps using mats and wedges can also enhance pathways.

- **Teepees**—create a quiet station along the way. Many children seek out places for time alone, and many simply enjoy private, hidden places (Wilson 1997). Use a teepee as a quiet place along an obstacle course where children can relax and take a break, or make a teepee the final destination on an obstacle course. Use wood board, PVC piping, and sturdy fabric. Provide water and a small snack in it. For greater aesthetic appeal, string sunflowers and ribbons around a teepee. Next to the teepee add a hammock for reading books. Set up a large beach umbrella next to it.

- **Straw bales** make wonderful obstacle-course mazes, flower beds, walls, and forts. Have you ever seen a straw-bale mountain? This is nothing more than secured, sequentially placed bales of straw for children to climb. Straw bales can be used as seating or for simple nook-and-cranny hideouts. Children enjoy sectioned-off landscaping that inspires big play ideas and "jumping-off" points. Use straw bales to square off obstacle-course play areas. Refer to the illustration below for a sectioned-off straw bale idea.

Nature Spark

Provide passive play opportunities on an obstacle course. Seats and perches allow children a chance to sit and watch birds or observe nature. Display a play crate or prop box full of periscopes, binoculars, telescopes, and compasses for children to explore (McGinnis 2002). Decks and playground patios can be used for block play or outdoor painting along an obstacle course.

STRAW BALE DISPLAY

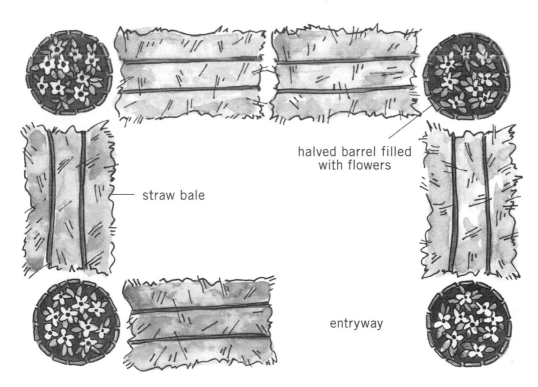

halved barrel filled with flowers

straw bale

entryway

Nature allows a child's imagination to thrive on play possibilities. Forts and castles with pretend princesses or fairies are what make childhood memorable. Hang old sheets from tree limbs or drape them over boxes to encourage a variety of play ideas. Encourage children to create their own play scenarios by offering a collection of sheets in many sizes, colors, and textures. Nurture such play adventures with storybooks and outdoor-adventure displays. Bamboo poles, planted flush with a school building, could ignite Jack and the Beanstalk pretend play. Surround the imaginative area with landscape fabric, mulch, bark, pebbles, and bean plants.

Nature Spark

Attach baskets to children's tricycles. This will allow them to stop and gather interesting and creative discoveries while pedaling through an obstacle course.

- **Old white sheets**, purchased or donated from charity stores, make great outdoor literacy or art walls. Hang sheets securely on a school wall. Allow children to paint on sheets with soupy mud and sand mixtures. Use wallpaper brushes, spray bottles, and sponges. Supply stepladders for children who want to create higher up on the sheet. Or spread sheets on a picnic table and let children write on them with bold-colored markers. Old sheets can be used as outdoor coverings to block out the sun and heat on especially warm days. Children can use white sheets and other fabrics to make shelters, capes, and royal robes. Give children paintbrushes in all sizes, and let them splat the sheet with mud—messy, but sensory stimulating.

- Nature has the potential to relax children. Use **picnic tables** to lure children to the calming beauty of nature. Situate a picnic table below a tree or beside a flower bed. Set up a listening center on one. Use a picnic table for an outside center to rotate a variety of meaningful and individualized manipulatives in color-coded bins. Manipulatives naturally encourage problem solving, making the activity an anytime, academically sound investment. Shoot for manipulatives that actively require the use of both hands.

- A large **pole** securely cemented into the ground can become an obstacle-course station for tetherball or maypole games. Two poles erected fairly close together could become a clothesline or curtains for an outdoor stage for dramatic skits, shows, and musical recitals. Add a large piece of carpet for stage flooring. Supply a karaoke machine and a play microphone for singing. Use wooden pallets and bread crates for building stage props. Fill a large box with accessories, such as hats, puppets, costumes, and jewelry.

- Colorful **rodeo-style barrels and cones**, situated as a tricycle-riding path, will supply endless physical play. Make courses curvy, zigzag, or bumpy with small mounds of sand to dodge. Set up flags and traffic signs for children to read and yield to. Make lanes to weave in and out of and stops, such as a lemonade stand or "trike wash." Have children take turns running the stops and riding the course. The beauty in a plain-colored cone or barrel is that it can become almost anything.

- Large **plastic tubs** make for great outdoor water play, especially bubble blowing with giant wands and digging and sifting through sensory items, such as leaves and seeds mixed with sand. A circle of large tubs, filled individually with mud, sand, water, and soft dirt, will create an individual play course. The possibilities for a sand circle are numerous. For example, fill tub 1 with soupy sand mixed with polished pebbles. Children can use pans as a sieve. Label the tub "#1 Gold Mining." Fill tub 2 with damp sand, buckets, and shovels. Fill tub 3 with fine colored sand mixed with flower petals, twigs, and shiny gems. The range of textures will be different for children, as soupy sand behaves differently than dry sand. Fill the tubs with soapy water and have children wash the classroom windows using an oversized sponge. Dry windows with a fluffy terrycloth towel. Cover tubs with a tarp when not in use.

OBSTACLE-COURSE STATIONS

The following stations are common to obstacle courses. Please consider safety, age appropriateness, and level of supervision at all times. Modify according to children's needs and interests. Add ropes, speaking funnels, mirror balls, pulleys, ladders, hanging prisms, and parachutes to liven up obstacle-course areas. Be sure to vary the scale of obstacles. For example, offer diminutive options, such as a sand pit with small doll furniture. Set out "just my size" chairs and tables, and don't forget the colossal versions, either! A big brass gong in the middle of the playground will prompt "larger than life" play. Successful obstacle courses offer children operational scales that open doors to their imagination and create play that screams "not only/but also" rather than "either/or" (Talbot and Frost 1989). Finally, don't forget the power of a little color. Use gold, silver, and copper enamels as well as traditional colors. Make courses sparkle, glitter, and shine!

- **Station 1: Playhouse**

  Outdoor playhouses can be kept simple by using several appliance boxes or made extravagant by using donated plywood and parental support. A wonderful point to keep in mind is that playhouses can have themes. Cardboard boxes can become an imaginative play cottage surrounded by a fence or border of alpine strawberries. Another idea: make a frontier fort

Nature Spark

Weave traditional games throughout the obstacle course. Some examples include Twister, musical chairs, freeze tag, red rover, hokey pokey, tug of war, egg-and-spoon races, hot potato, leapfrog, and red light/green light.

Imaginative play can be supported easily with simple nature props and donated items. A large bucket filled with mud balls and grass could be labeled "Crock-Pot" in a playhouse kitchen. Natural herbs and plants can be pretend stews and magical potions in playhouse kitchens. A large box full of sparkly gems and polished pebbles could be labeled as frontier gold!

complete with log fence and thinly sliced logs laid out as a path to the playhouse. Creativity combined with student interest will ensure a successful outdoor playhouse along an obstacle course.

- **Station 2: Discovery Trail**

  A discovery trail on an obstacle course combines the use of tires, balance beams, mats, hula hoops, and carpet squares to create a play trail through which children can jump, roll, and maneuver. Pattern the trail to keep curiosity and wonderment high. Situate the discovery trail near flower gardens, water fountains, and bug-attracting bushes to spark side investigations.

- **Station 3: Sensory Pit**

  A sensory pit is an integral part of an outdoor obstacle course. To a young child it is a sensory smorgasbord. Fill plastic swimming pools with stimulating balls and fabric of various colors and textures. Nub balls are fantastic for outdoor sensory pits. Children can squeeze, roll, throw, and kick them. Chunked fabric choices to fill a sensory pit may include burlap, silk, corduroy, and terry cloth.

- **Station 4: Tunnel Play**

  Children enjoy playing in and running through outdoor tunnels. A tunnel on an obstacle course can provide an entry into a playhouse. Tunnels offer stimulating physical play and allow children to generate their own play. Put balls inside the tunnel. Stick bubble wrap to tunnel flooring—the sound will surprise children as they crawl through the tunnel. Place two tunnels together and have tunnel races for added exercise. Plastic trash cans and large appliance boxes with their bottoms cut out make great tunnels too.

- **Station 5: Cable-Spool Tables**

  The purpose of cable-spool tables is to allow children to do things outdoors that are normally done indoors. For example, a cable table situated in a dirt-and-sand area could display plastic tubs full of blocks in all shapes and sizes. Such a table could provide hours of play for children. Other cable-spool-table ideas include a painting table, a listening table with audiobooks and headphones, or a washing cable table next to a water spigot with several buckets of water, wash rags, soap bars, baby dolls, and clothes for washing. Cable-spool tables are easy to set up and tear down—simply clear the top and roll to storage.

- **Station 6: Clothesline**

  An outdoor clothesline can provide a variety of activities to stimulate children's interests. Construct a clothesline using cement, poles, and a drying line. The cement should be sunk underground. Make sure that cemented poles allow the clothesline to fasten low enough for children to hang clothes on but high enough to prevent injuries. Make wind chimes out of berry baskets, old CDs, beads, and spools. Hang chimes from the clothesline on blustery days. Cover stale bagels and donuts with peanut butter and birdseed and hang from the clothesline with colored yarn. Have children watch for visiting birds. Play ball games, similar to tennis and volleyball, where children throw balls over or under the line (Thompson 1994). Use a variety of balls, including Koosh and Ping-Pong balls. Let children paint wooden craft clothespins, decorate them as animals, and hang them from the clothesline.

- **Station 7: Mud Hole**

  Making a big, messy mud hole and playing in it is a childhood rite of passage. Mud play encourages scientific, hands-on exploration! Using large buckets, shovels, and a garden hose, let children create a mucky mud pit on warm days. Make sure it doesn't get too deep! And be certain to supervise the play. Allow students to put on oversized galoshes and stomp and romp around. Make plungers (specifically for mud-hole play) available. The possibilities for play props are limitless. Supply toy vehicles, dinosaurs, blocks, and donated bread and milk crates to construct bridges. Although untidy, a mud hole provides fabulous sensory integration! Use a garden hose to clean children off after mud-hole play.

Closing Thoughts

For healthy play stage development, children require diversity and sensory stimulation in an environment with developmentally appropriate practice (Wilson 1997). As more children are growing up in urban environments, the need for nature-oriented, developmentally appropriate classrooms grows more pressing. Opportunities for immediate encounters with nature should remain at the forefront of a classroom rich in developmentally appropriate practice. Children running, jumping, skipping, and shrieking with joyous laughter while outdoors are signs that active participation in nature is unfolding. Children are terrific at making extraordinary things out of ordinary things. Incorporating easy, hands-on experiments and nature-oriented learning centers will allow nature connections across the classroom curriculum. Nature field trips, hikes, and obstacle courses all aid in offering students a more nature-oriented classroom curriculum. A classroom environment with multisensory, nature-driven experiences will not only bring children closer to the natural world, but instill an appreciation for it as well.

Using Nature to Create Special Play Places

Children between birth and six years old explore their surroundings best and take in knowledge best through their senses, so they benefit from activities that involve direct contact with nature (Humphryes 2000). Consider this example of a simple, spontaneous, and unguided nature activity. Place a nature box—a printer paper box or a large shoe box filled with fascinating and mysterious items, such as a mushroom coral, rattling gourd, acorn, obsidian, oyster shell, even a shriveled-up lizard!—on a stump outside for children to look through during free play. Then watch as the box invariably sparks spontaneous, developmentally appropriate play among them.

Try to pump up outdoor play places for aspiring or timid naturalists. The nature-driven ideas that follow will spark your imagination, especially as you see the benefits of providing ample time outdoors for child-driven play. They will also show you how to implement developmentally appropriate outdoor play activities with objectives directly linked to nature:

- to understand the power and importance of play in the natural world to bring out a child's inner nature lover

- to use natural elements to create powerful play opportunities in and out of the classroom

- to present examples of special outdoor play places, seats, stages, and lofts for children to nurture their inner nature lover

. . . .

The Power and Importance of Play in Nature

Susan Isaacs, in *Social Development in Children* (1946, 425), states, "Play is not only the means by which the child comes to discover the world; it is supremely the activity which brings him psychic equilibrium in the early years." Play is a vital component to the healthy development of children. It is not only their work, but also what they require to learn. Early education pioneer Lev Vygotsky considered play the highest level of development for young children. Through play, children develop in the areas of creativity, problem solving, logic, social skills, and language acquisition. According to Henderson and Atencio (2007, 246), "play allows children to try behaviors, thoughts, experiences, roles, and skills out at a level above their normal cognitive level." As you ponder ideas for play places and special spaces, remember that a child's play environment should encourage nature play while maintaining a focus on the experience and learning process. Nature play should also challenge the child to inquire about more. For example, when children make adobe bricks using dirt, water, and sand, they are not only connected to the sensory thrill of mixing dirt, water, and sand, but also to the amazing history of adobe brick making. American Indians in the Southwest used sun-baked bricks to build their homes. After children make their own bricks, prompting questions connect nature and learning:

- What made the bricks so hard?

- How did the bricks dry so quickly?

- How do bricks keep an adobe home so warm?

An activity such as this one will satisfy quality experiences and exploration largely because the child will be encouraged to investigate the materials in many ways, including through actions and questions (Henderson and Atencio 2007). Allow students to use as many or all their senses within the activity as possible. In doing so, children will have an easier time learning and retaining the information presented to them.

. . . .

Use Natural Elements to Play

The natural world is full of simple surprises. Roll a heavy log over after a long winter or peek in a beech-tree hole in the early spring. By using water, dirt, sand, dew, and rain, children are encouraged to explore and interact with the natural world while their curiosity expands their imagination and invents more robust play.

Nature is, without a doubt, its own curriculum. Nature-driven lessons allow you to teach children less and guide more by using open-ended questions to spark further investigation—"Why do you think there are so many bugs under this big log?" Your role as an educator is to continue modeling enthusiasm within play. Share your wonder and nurture *their* curiosity. Follow student cues by observing and listening closely as they interact with the natural world and its elements, which is the first step to bringing them closer to nature. Consider the following natural elements to prompt outdoor play.

Water

Oceans, beaches, rivers, lakes, and puddles—water is a powerful natural medium for helping children learn. Water can be studied as a pourable liquid, frozen solid as ice cubes, or vaporized on a Bunsen burner. The added bonus of water play being fantastic sensory play is icing on the cake. Water can be colored, scented, thickened, and bubbled for children's play. *Water Dance* by Thomas Locker and *Water* by Frank Asch are marvelous books that introduce water in several breathtaking nature settings. When you feel children have familiarity working informally with water, such as at a water table with cups and funnels, move on to nature forms, such as rain, dew, fog, frost, snow, ponds, and tap water.

After a rainfall take students outside to look for rainbows. Ask students why they think a rainbow appeared. Pass out prisms and crystals and view the rainbows. Comment on the colors.

Children love playing with bubbles. A super-sized bubble recipe for super-sized bubble play is available in chapter 4. Another bubble play idea: fill a large bucket with water and a few teaspoons of dish soap. Set out a variety of eggbeaters or whisks for children to froth bubbles.

RAIN

The outdoors is most alive and alert when wet. Rain is a natural element with tremendous opportunities: it can be felt, smelled, tasted, heard, and seen. Discuss how our beautiful world would dry out without rain. Flowers, trees, animals, and land require rain to live and thrive. Collect rainwater in several buckets and compare it to tap water. Discuss the differences. Additional rainy-day activities include the following.

Play in the Rain: On a misty but warm day, let children fidget and frolic outdoors. Collect an assortment of umbrellas, windbreakers, ponchos, galoshes, and raincoats for appropriate outerwear. Playing in light rain showers is safe as long as children are dressed appropriately and are not shivering, and, of course, as long as there is no lightning. When it rains on spring afternoons and the raindrops are big and warm, let children run around briefly without their shoes and socks.

Puddle Play: Playing in rain puddles is a blast! Children love it. After a heavy rainfall or while it is misting, let students put on galoshes and venture outside to romp and stomp in puddles. Scatter leaves and rocks in fresh patches of rain, and let children scoop them out with their hands or small nets (see net making on page 92). Ask students why the leaves float in the puddles and the rocks do not. Read *Red Rubber Boot Day* by Mary Lyn Ray, a beautifully illustrated book, to end the activity.

Trike Riding: Pull out small tricycles and wagons while it is sprinkling outside. The friction from the pedaling will cause water to splash up onto the children—a sensation most will enjoy; they may pedal harder and faster for more! Have children ride their trikes and pull their wagons on a variety of surfaces in the wet weather. Try grass, sand, and asphalt for different muscle work and resistance. Make curvy and zigzag paths.

Bubble Play: Children enjoy blowing bubbles anytime and anywhere. During a light rain shower, the activity is more challenging. Add baking soda and vinegar to the bubble solution for more frothy and fizzy bubbles. An idea for vocabulary expansion: discuss with students the many ways they can use the bubbly water. It can be *blown* through a wand, *sprayed* from a big bottle, *splashed* from a dish, *squeezed* from a rag, and *dripped* from an eyedropper.

Digging: Pull out an assortment of child-sized shovels and pails. Let children dig deep in sand or dirt while light rain showers fall. Dirt and sand are softer and easier to manipulate when damp. Plus, worms and other insects often venture to the top of wet soil. Children will be amazed by the unexpected wiggly surprises. Other rain digging ideas: make mud pies together after you have dug a small mound of dirt. Create roadways in the wet soil and pull out small vehicles or big trucks for children to push, pull, and "vroom" through the sand while light showers fall.

Make a Moat: When the forecast calls for light rain, make a moat with children in the sandbox. Add to the activity by making sieves. Poke holes in various recyclable items or foil containers—plates, bowls, cups, or fast-food packaging. Let children observe how the water drips, flows, or streams through sieves.

DEW

Dew is an element of nature that is not only beautiful, but also mysterious. Conditions have to be just right for dew to do its thing. Discuss such special conditions with children. Pitara Kids Network (www.pitara.com) simplifies them well: "When a warm and clear day is followed by a cool evening and night, which is clear (cloudless), dew is formed." Children will delight in dew discovery and the shared experience of feeling it between their fingers on a brisk morning.

Dew Up Close: When morning activities are nearing break time, dress appropriately and venture outside with magnifying glasses to look closely at dewdrops up close. This activity can be done before or after a scheduled circle time. Read a connecting story when you return to class. Discuss what you observed. Have students write or draw their observations in a nature journal on your return indoors.

Dew Walk: Inform parents in a newsletter that you will be going on a dew walk as a class. Children will need to bring in a pair of old tennis shoes and an extra pair of socks for the stroll. For the walk, have students change into their spare shoes. Walk through grass or any natural, lush playground area. Ask children what is happening to their shoes as they move through the

Nature Spark

Another simple rain idea is to demonstrate how rain occurs. Boil water in a teakettle or on a Bunsen burner. Above the boiling water, hold a pot full of ice cubes. Children will observe steam and drops of rain dripping from the sides of the pot (Crawford et al. 2009). Discuss with students what they see.

Nature Spark

Discuss with students the differences between raindrops and dewdrops. Raindrops fall from above. Dewdrops form on the ground. A wonderful resource to invest in is the book *Exploring Water with Young Children* by Ingrid Chalufour and Karen Worth. Visit www.redleafpress.org for details.

dew. Are they getting wet? Why? Extend the activity by having the children walk on dew-covered leaves. Ask how the leaves sound when they are walked on. Are they brittle and crunchy sounding? Have students smell the wet leaves. How do they smell? Have them reflect on the walk in their nature journal.

FOG AND FROST

Like dew, fog and frost are puzzling elements of nature that will challenge a child's perception and observation skills. Simply defined, fog is a cloud that touches the ground, while frost is frozen water crystals on a cold surface. An activity follows for each.

Fog Calling: On an especially foggy morning, dress children appropriately and take them outside. Line half the students on one side of the playground and the other half on the other side. Have students take turns calling out to each other. See if they can decipher who called out to whom. Roll a big ball back and forth across the fog to each side. Have students try and guess who caught the ball. Discuss with students why they are not able to see each other. Define *fog* for them and let them walk around in it. Not many picture books deal with fog, but *Hide and Seek Fog* by Alvin Tresselt does so magnificently. Make it available in your class library.

Frosty Letters: On a chilly morning when frost is evident on your classroom windows, allow students to draw pictures or write their names on the windows. Talk with them about what causes frost to form. If snow begins to fall, extend the activity by asking, "Why do you think it is snowing?" Take students outside (dressed appropriately) to view frost with a magnifying glass. Feel the frost for differences on the ground, grass, or sand.

SNOW

Winter has a wonderfully white and wet characteristic—snow! Snow is a magical substance to explore. It melts and ices over as well as turns slushy. Snow discussion questions are vast: How does the grass survive when snow blankets it? What causes snow to fall? A wonderful children's classic to file for story time is *The Snowy Day* by Ezra Jack Keats. Let children venture online to research W. A. "Snowflake" Bentley, a famous photographer of snowflakes. His work is displayed in museums across the nation

Nature Spark

Create fog with your students. This activity is one you perform and children observe. It's easy! Materials include a clear plastic bottle, hot water, ice, and rubbing alcohol. Fill the bottle about one-third full of hot water. Add several drops of alcohol. Have students watch closely as the alcohol vaporizes quickly. Place a piece of ice over the bottle mouth. Once again, have children observe what happens near the neck of the bottle. Hint: fog will appear!

and can be found in his book *Snow Crystals*. The following are more snow activities. Always ensure that children are appropriately dressed for cold weather.

Sledding: After a snowfall, take students outside for a short time. Let them push and pull a variety of sleds, such as snow saucers. Homemade cardboard versions with secured rope are also fun. Set out child-sized shovels for children to scoop and swivel the snow. Be sure to dress warmly.

Snow Sculptures: After a heavy snowfall, venture outside to build snow sculptures and igloos. Supply an assortment of items, such as carrots, hats, branches, and scarves, for embellishing snow people or animals. If you are fortunate to have snowdrifts, let students study them. Have them look closely and compare the top of the drift to the bottom of the drift. What do they see?

Catch Snowflakes: During a brisk snowfall, take students outside to catch snowflakes on their tongues. Black card stock can also be used to catch snowflakes; simply have students hold out the paper before them. The flakes will be more visible against the black paper. See page 102 for a yummy candy recipe featuring fresh-fallen snow.

Hunt for Tracks: Look for animal tracks in the snow. If you find a track or two, have students draw them in a nature journal. Have students try to identify the track. Another idea: search for abandoned bird nests in the snow.

Measure the Depth of a Snowfall: After a vigorous snowfall, take students outside to measure the snow with rulers and yardsticks. This is an excellent time to incorporate a mini lesson on measurement instruments and their uses. Discuss a metric stick, a measuring tape, a thermometer, a barometer, and other scales or instruments.

Examine Ice Puddles: Light winter snow and rain showers can produce small ice puddles. Allow students to examine the rare combination by cracking the tops with sticks and stones. If proper attire is worn, stomping on one can be quite satisfying to children.

Nature Spark

Depending on the length of Jack Frost's annual visit, making a snow house or fortress wall with children is doable. Snow blocks can be made using sturdy plastic boxes as molds. Spray down with cooking spray to remove blocks without breaking. The film *Nanook of the North* is a great resource for igloo making.

PONDS

Installing a small pond in a child care setting is a wonderful way to promote multisensory, nature-oriented water play. An inexpensive pond kit can quickly transform a play yard into a greener and more inviting play space. Ponds are a refreshing refuge for little critters; add inexpensive annuals for more appeal, as well as a hose or sprinkler waterfall, a bridge, or stepping-stones textured with imprinted leaves. Please note: all water areas and activities with young children must always be properly supervised.

Simple small pond ideas include the following:

Tadpole and Algae Pond: Fill a tot-sized pond with tadpoles for children to observe and chart their growth from polliwog to frog. Discuss how the wiggly babies grow into frogs. Keep an eye out for moss growth. Let students retrieve a wad of moss with a craft stick. Place the moss in a jar and observe with a magnifying glass. Allow eager naturalists to wear nonlatex gloves while they feel and smell the algae. Take time to discuss why children should not taste specimens. Let students clean out leaves from the pond with small aquarium nets. Discuss sensory reactions. Create a natural-looking fence for a tadpole-algae pond using large tree branches that have been stripped and bound tightly together with heavy twine. Thick branches that have been cut into short stumps can also be used. Have students gather the fencing material. A tadpole pond can even welcome a turtle during the warmer months of the year.

Snail Pond: Let students observe water snails with a magnifying glass in a tiny pond area. Remove a snail or two from the pond and place in a small jar for students to observe up close. Discuss how snails slither up the jar sides. Then let students toss small pebbles in the pond to see if they can make ripples. Ask them what causes the water to react. Explore other wet habitats, such as beaver ponds and marshes.

What Makes a Pond a Pond? Sitting around your school pond, discuss different bodies of water: a pond, lake, river, bog, ocean, puddle, and canal. Allow students to draw similarities and differences in their nature journal. Talk about what makes a pond a pond. Here are several points about ponds to "ponder" with children. The questions are taken from the *Ponds for Kids Activity Guide* (Aquascape 2011) found online at www .aquascapeinc.com. Tailor questions to suit your students and your class pond project.

1. The water temperature is the same at the bottom and top of ponds. Does our pond have the same water temperature at the bottom and top? What would you use to figure this out?

2. Ponds are never deeper than twenty feet. Is our pond less than twenty feet deep? What would you use to figure this out?

3. Ponds always have smooth surfaces and never have waves even on windy days. Is our pond surface smooth and without waves even on windy days? How would we figure this out?

Three more forms of water to discuss with children are clouds, hail, and tears. Depending on the age of your students, all could generate additional water activities and ideas.

Soil

I once heard a professor compare the early years of a child's life to soil, suggesting that the young years must be cultivated like rich soil and sown with seeds of wonder and movement. Allowing children the chance to dig deeply and explore soil will spark learning. Soil is a great multisensory tool because it can be offered to children in a variety of ways—as chunky mud for making pies, dry dirt clods for hammering apart, moist clay for sculpting, or extrafine sand for sifting through funnels. Soil is available in various shades. It is everywhere and never in short supply. Activities that feature soil follow.

DIRT

As a child I lived in Kansas, Oklahoma, Virginia, and New Mexico. One distinct feature of each state is dirt. Oklahoma dirt was very red and stained my play clothes easily. Kansas dirt was thin and dusty and drifted indoors daily, where it landed

Nature Spark

Implement a duck unit while studying ponds. Ducks are mysterious to observe on ponds. They appear to be gliding unruffled and sailing smoothly. Yet under the water their webbed feet are paddling away. Have students compare and contrast ducks and geese, especially their sounds and flying patterns. Introduce a simple Venn diagram as a visual to compare the two species. Have students draw the graph comparison in their nature journals.

on windowsills. My chores called for keeping it out! Virginia dirt was black, thick, moist, and full of big, fat worms and slugs, which my older brothers collected. New Mexico dirt is dry and full of sharp stickers referred to as goatheads. Regardless of dirt color or texture, children enjoy discovering worms, roots, and rocks, as well as making dirt soup, dirt pie, and "hot chocolate." Set out chunky trucks with big scoops for driving in dirt mounds. Dirt can act as an instant drawing board for quick games of tic-tac-toe, hopscotch, hangman, or spelling practice. Here are other dirt activities to try:

Nature Spark

Plants cater wonderfully to all of a child's senses—color, texture, fragrance, and softness. Below is a handy chart with plant suggestions for gardening and planting with children. Use the chart to decorate play places, special spaces, seats, and stages, which are presented beginning on page 78.

Plant Flowers: A simple activity to get children digging and exploring dirt is to plant flowers with them. Digging deep in dirt and breaking up soil clods with child-sized trowels is a great sensory experience. Let children jump on freshly dug dirt with their bare feet and piggies! Plant flowers in each color of the rainbow for a lovely, educational, rainbow-colored flower garden. Start with simple flowers, such as marigolds and zinnias. Sunflowers are terrific too; children will marvel at their height. While planting flowers with children, take time to have them look inside the flower and feel its petals and leaves. Children do eventually need to be introduced to basic flower parts, but even more so they need to learn why a flower is so beautiful. Ask students why they enjoy looking at a flower and smelling it.

Plants that cater to all senses	Lamb's ears (cool texture!), sage, chives, mint, dianthus, sweet peas, zinnias, basil, poppies, baby's breath, pansies, petunias, and alyssum
Simple fruit and vegetable plants	Cherry tomatoes, peas, string beans, melons, carrots, potatoes, beets, popcorn, sweet corn, broccoli, and lettuce *Note*: Overplant to ensure children are allowed optimal "harvesting" experiences.
Plants that attract insects (butterflies, ladybugs)—**even bunnies and frogs!**	Phlox, chocolate mint, dill, parsley, hollyhocks, milkweed, butterfly bushes, salvia, asters, trumpet vine, cosmos, and impatiens

(Torquati and Barber 2005)

Dive into Dirt Hills: Children love to dig in dirt. Exploratory, archaeology-bound dirt digging is a childhood favorite. If possible, create a variety of dirt hills for children to climb on and dig holes in. Bury plastic worms and bugs, twigs, acorns, and other little treasures for a sensory explosion. See page 115 for toss-ins. Give each child a treasure-finding kit that includes a child-sized hand shovel to dig with and a paintbrush to dust off discoveries. Put both items, along with a small pad and chunky crayon, in a medium-sized plastic bag. Enjoy the earthy scent of dirt with children too.

Magnify Dirt: Set out an assortment of magnifying glasses and age-appropriate microscopes on an outdoor table. Let children snoop around on the ground with the magnifying glasses. Assist them in making dirt slides to view under the microscopes. Discuss what they see. Have them draw any dirt observations in their nature journals.

Make Dirt Bricks: This activity is especially sensory-oriented. Children love it! You'll need an old plastic coffee container, dirt (to turn into fine mud), sand, water, and several sturdy shoe boxes. To make adobe bricks with students, mix four coffee cans full of fine mud. For every four cans of mud, mix one coffee can full of sand. Let children manipulate the mixture until it balls up and does not crack. Pack the brick mixture into a shoe box and set it in the sun for three to four days. Rip the box off the brick when dried. For round adobe bricks, fill a metal coffee can halfway. For mini bricks, fill ice cube trays with the mixture. Visit www.beniciahistoricalmuseum.org /tours/edu_hands.htm for additional information on adobe bricks and homes.

CLAY

Natural clay is unlike dirt, sand, or mud in that it starts out cool but becomes malleable and warms to the temperature of a child's hands. Dry, cracking clay on a child's hands will ignite questions and catapult further exploration. Good-quality clay can be a sensory explosion, especially if it smells fresh from a riverbed. Children will enjoy rolling, smearing, smashing, and coiling it. Children will enjoy pressing nature items, such as seeds and rocks, into fresh clay. Additional clay activities include the following:

Nature Spark

Keep your students safe! Be well aware of unsafe plants, herbs, and flowers. Contact your local poison-control agency or get a complete and accurate list of all toxic plants in your area. Even common plants such as morning glories are highly toxic (Torquati and Barber 2005). When an unsafe plant is discovered, use it as a teachable moment. Explain to children why the plant is not to be bothered.

Nature Spark

A wonderful clay resource for early childhood educators is *I Am Clay*, a must-see DVD (also in VHS) that demonstrates the benefits of working with natural clay, which enhances children's emotional, creative, intellectual, and physical development.

Nature Spark

To learn more about clay play for children, check out Clay Talk, a free, interactive online community. Visit www.k-play .com/clay.

Nature Spark

For proper clay storage, wrap in a tablecloth and tie up at the ends with a rope. This allows the clay to stay moist and readily available (Rogers and Steffan 2009).

Pottery: Clay play is perfect at a picnic table. Children can tear pieces from a big block. Place several small bowls of water on a tablecloth for children to make pottery. Demonstrate coiling the material in the shape of bowls, candleholders, and dishes. Show students how to roll skinny snakes, pinch fat pots, hammer clumps with their hands, or hollow out ornamental creations with a popsicle stick. For clay play, avoid obvious gadgets, such as rolling pins and cookie cutters. Leave children alone with their imaginations to plunge into the natural medium.

Sensory-Table Clay Play: Change the consistency of clay by placing it in an outdoor sensory table filled with a little water. Vary its texture. Make it bumpy, rough, sandy, or smooth. Let children experiment with various clay colors such as white, red, or gray. At the sensory table, let children explore the medium while blindfolded on a cool spring day. Listening to nature sounds in the background while playing is also a wonderful idea. *Moods of Nature* offers sounds from the woods, rain forest, and tropics. Clay exploration can also be kept simple: fill a bucket and leave it next to the sandbox for children to investigate.

SAND

Whether it is warm and wet from the beach or hot and dry from the desert, sand is fabulous for outdoor sensory play. Sandboxes or sandpits with easy access are one of the best ways to accommodate sand play. Oversized tires filled with sand are great for seated sand play. Finger drawing in a tray full of sand, in a variety of colors and textures, is a simple sand activity for students. Pump up outside sand play by adding water to the experience, as well as providing sturdy plastic cups, bowls, old kitchen strainers, funnels, spoons, and other retired kitchen utensils. Here are additional sand play ideas:

Sand Cookies: Scatter an assortment of cookie cutters in sand. Moisten the sand for a more intense "cooking" experience. Scatter seashells and pebbles in sand for a make-believe beach adventure. Sprinkle fine, colored sand for variety, or place in old salt-and-pepper shakers and allow children to decorate their "cookies."

Buried Treasure: Bury small toys that children can dig up. Make a map leading to where "X" marks the spot. Hide ice cubes in sand as well. Let children walk through sand with their eyes closed to discover chilling sensations.

Sand Games: Teach children to draw in the sand with a stick—or play tic-tac-toe. Create roads and moats for toy cars, boats, and trucks.

Sand Weighing: Place several metric scales on sturdy boxes if tables or a flat surface are not available. Offer children foam containers for weighing sand or mud projects. Set out a variety of nature specimens—such as large pinecones, twigs, acorns, and shells of all shapes and sizes—to weigh and compare.

Screen Sifting: Situate an old screen over several plastic crates for sifting play. Make holes in different sizes through which to sift sand, water, and flour!

MUD AND MORE

The joy of making traditional mud pies also provides sensory stimulation through hands-on play. And the only thing more pleasurable than jumping in a rain puddle is getting dirty in a *mud* puddle! Whether making mucky pies in disposable trays at an outdoor bakery or sculpting castles in a mud pit, children seldom tire of messing around in mud. They delight in squishing their toes in mud as well. More activities include the following:

Mud Sensory Table: Vary the texture of mud at an outdoor sensory table. Make it thick and clumpy, or add sand so it is gritty. Children like to play in mud soup, which is thin mud mixed with various toss-ins (see page 115). Add a variety of toys and containers to accompany a mud sensory table.

Mud Murals: Turn an outside area into one that caters to mud painting. Situate a large sheet on the side of the school building or attach large pieces of paper to easels. Make mud paint in a variety of textures: smooth, thick, creamy, or runny with bits of dry leaves, grass blades, hay strands, and a few shakes of sand and salt. Two wonderful children's books that add to a muddy nature lesson include *Mud* by Mary Lyn Ray and *Pigs in the Mud in the Middle of the Rud* by Lynn Plourde.

Composting: Composting is a wonderful cross-curriculum exercise. Children will learn about much more than just decomposition. Safely and securely erect a boxed-in compost bin that will

Nature Spark

Sand has incredible sensory possibilities. Shop online for an assortment of natural and artificial sands. Aqua Sand is specially formulated to look and feel like real dry sand—even when just scooped out of water! Jurassic Sand is superclean, reusable sand, which is great for children with allergies. Quicksand is clean quartz sand requiring only water to turn it into crumbly sandstone. Sandtastik is white play sand that is ideal for indoor sand tables. Moon Sand molds to any shape imaginable. Space Sand never gets wet in water and is similar in color and composition to soil from Mars. Tropical play sand is safe and durable for children's indoor or outdoor play. Talk with children about the properties of different kinds of sand.

generate many worthwhile lessons in science and mathematics. Children will enjoy gathering dried leaves, pine needles, grass clippings, weeds, and other scraps to add to the bin. In a newsletter, encourage parents to send students to school with tightly wrapped items that can be dumped into the class compost pile. Suitable materials include recyclable newsprint, coffee grounds, and kitchen vegetable scraps. *Compost, By Gosh!* by Michelle Eva Portman makes a wonderful resource book for your classroom library. Robert E. (Skip) Richter, CEA-Horticulture, Travis County, Texas Agricultural Extension Service, has presented a detailed and scripted lesson on composting. Visit the following website: http://aggie-horticulture .tamu.edu/kindergarden/kidscompost/cover.html.

Worm Bin: Nurturing a child's curiosity about small creatures that creep, crawl, leap, and wriggle can help them overcome nature fears. To make a worm bin, fill a large metal stock tank with mud and a variety of earthworms, snails, beetles, and crickets in all sizes (Rosenow 2008). Offer shovels, gardening gloves, and pails for children to use when exploring and digging in the bin, as well as sticky gloves (see page 103 for making sticky gloves). Worm bins and farms can be set up indoors or out. Never force a child to play in the worm bin if he appears timid or openly expresses disinterest. For children who are not comfortable with creepy-crawly insects, introduce plastic bugs and worms at the sensory or manipulative table. Set out picture books with realistic bugs. *Wonderful Worms* by Linda Glaser is a perfect choice for learning about underground friends. Let timid children view bugs, such as grasshoppers and ladybugs, in homemade bug houses (Torquati and Barber 2005). See page 91 for making bug houses.

Nature Spark

Earthworms are fascinating to observe and study. Here are a few fun worm facts and activities to share with students. Worms eat their way through soil by squeezing and stretching. Bristles on earthworms help them move through soil. Use a magnifying glass to observe worm bristles. Let students listen to worms. Place one in a small brown paper bag and put your ear up close. Do you hear a scratching sound? Shine a flashlight on an earthworm. What does it do? (Hauser 1998).

Special Nature Play Places, Seats, Stages, and Lofts

Children enjoy special and intimate places to engage freely in pretend play. The outdoors is the perfect place for creating natural play environments for children, regardless of the season.

The decor and themes are vast. As you contemplate ideas for these spaces, ask for student input and interests. As Lisa Miles (2009, 41) advocates, "Whatever the play space becomes, we must remember to keep the environment the children's and to fill it with interesting and beautiful things." The experience becomes more meaningful and brings truth to Alice Sterling Honig's (2007, 78) words, "Play deepens a child's sense of serenity and joy." The success of any outdoor play area depends on the following factors:

1. The play setting should have clear boundaries and be well stocked with materials that children can easily access. Children should be able to clean up and put things away by themselves.

2. Although outside, the nature play environment should have order. Rules—and consequences for not following them—should be enforced.

3. The play space should be as authentic and attractive looking as possible. For example, one of the first special play places discussed is an outdoor play center with an old-time general store theme. To give children a realistic sense of a general store, stock it as true to pioneering and homesteading times as possible. Place "olden-day" items, such as canisters, blankets, and colorful print fabrics, in the store. To get a feel for the general-store theme, refer to the *My First Little House Book* series by Laura Ingalls Wilder (Miles 2009). I suggest leaving several of the books in the play center for children to read and view the illustrations.

When creating special places, remember one additional point: present the play place and its materials, then get out of the way. Let the children take over to discover, explore, and maneuver their way through the special place at their own pace and in their own way. Educators often assume they need to explain and show constantly. Children gain as much, maybe even more, when they are allowed uninterrupted time to mingle, interact, and *play* freely with one another in a way and space all their own (Miles 2009). Children "seem to know innately how to appreciate and live in the joyous moments, if only we allow them to do so" (Ginsburg and Jablow 2006, 121).

The following ideas are for creating special nature-oriented play places, seats, stages, and lofts for children's outdoor enjoyment and curriculum expansion. They will help bring out the nature lover in your students, preserve their childhood curiosity, and spark an ongoing desire to explore.

Play Places

The outdoor setting allows for new perspectives in play, especially if a special place has been created for imaginative play. Nature paths, thick grass, and unique tracks are wonderful additions to play areas that can cultivate play opportunities. Wide open play spaces allow for story enhancement as well as physical activity. Childhood is about play through imagination; a special play place nurtures exploration and encourages curiosity.

Logs Path: Walking and balancing on a connected circular log path surrounded by natural herbs, such as spearmint, peppermint, and chocolate mint, can make for a pleasurable play place. Add nature sounds—CDs of wind, rain, and even thunder! Scatter bark chunks, wood chips, or straw in the center of the log circle. Use natural landforms with a variety of textures such as mulch and grass to your advantage as you place the logs. Erect a homemade railing for children with special needs. Include a shrub that children can search for leaves or bugs. It can also be a hiding place. Add a big rock for children to climb on. Leave outdoor prop boxes (see page 18) on the logs. Large play logs beckon balancing, jumping, bark rubbing, bug hunting, bark stripping, ring counting, and playing follow the leader (Keeler 2008). A quick tip: make sure that the natural specimens are not sterile looking and unrealistic, which will discourage further nature investigation. And remember, even a rotting log can be examined by students under close supervision.

Tire Tracks: Construct a tire trail for play. Systematically lay out three to four tires, each filled with a variety of nature-oriented items and sensory "stuff"—soupy sand filled with toss-ins (see page 115), for example, and linking toys. Fill another tire with small containers of nature items, such as acorns, nuts, seedpods, and shells, that can be used to make jewelry (see page 96 for an explanation of nature jewelry). Designate a third tire as a mud-pie-making center. Old car or tractor

Nature Spark

Invite butterflies to play places by setting out overly ripe fruit, such as bananas and pears, on old, colorful plastic plates. Set them in play places where children can observe the flying guests. Butterflies also enjoy sipping muddy water. Set out several Frisbees full of muddy water. Add pebbles and twigs for butterflies to perch on while drinking.

tires can be used. Be aware that rubber tires contain volatile organic compounds (VOCs) and may also contain heavy metals. To prevent exposure to these hazards, be sure tires are not torn or crumbling. Clean the tires and make sure they're free from glass, nails, and other foreign objects, and drill holes in the tires to release rainwater. Then give the tires a new look with a coat of bright paint.

When using tires in children's play, remember to position the tires so they don't accumulate rainwater; standing water can be a source of mosquito breeding.

Old Barrels: Large, clean plastic barrels can be turned into tunnels or situated accordingly for more entertaining play possibilities. Children can use clean barrels to roll around on the playground. Barrels can be cut in half and turned into ponds or a water trough for supervised play.

Old Rowboats and Canoes: Bury an old rowboat or canoe in the ground. Add creative accessories, such as play fishing poles, nets (see page 92 for a net-making activity), and tackle boxes full of rubber worms and sensory sorts. Mount a wheel off an old stroller (preferably a large all-terrain wheel) as a steering wheel for a pirate adventure. Don't forget the telescope and a "walking" plank! Another idea: make a wooden raft out of donated two-by-fours. Mark Twain's classic *The Adventures of Huckleberry Finn* has several realistic illustrations of rafts and canoes to show and explain to children.

Lush Lawn: Mow a tic-tac-toe board into a grassy area. The large-scale game is a fantastic idea for physical play. Use hula hoops and jump ropes to mark game play spots. Make sure to plant hearty grass that can stand a beating! Another idea: in the fall, craft a trail of crisp fallen leaves on a lawn for children to run through. Rustling leaves are not only pleasurable to feel, but amazing to hear. Dampen the leaves for a more physical activity (dry leaves are not as heavy as wet leaves).

Mini Orchard: Small fruit trees can create an enchanted orchard for children to play in. Plant a variety of other textured plants for children to explore, such as snapdragons, bleeding hearts, or prickly strawflowers. Offer blankets and picnic sets, small baskets, step stools (to reach and explore in the trees), and crates of play items, such as dolls, tea sets, and chunky trucks. Add several large rocks or logs; hide a hose and trickle water down the side. From a child's perspective, it is a forest or a magical grove. Read *Gathering the Sun: An Alphabet in Spanish and English* by Alma Flor Ada to students. It welcomes children into orchards and introduces the people who work in them. Discuss the gentle and constant care of "baby" fruit trees. Other ideas: plant a pumpkin patch in the summer that children can enjoy and observe in the fall. Strawberry patches are delightful to children as well.

Mazes: Cornstalks and large sunflowers can be planted to create a maze. Both are hearty, fast-growing plants that can easily define, shade, and accent outdoor play place walls and boundaries. Although sunflowers attract insects such as bees, they are suitable for play places. Supervise and modify according to student activity level. Climbing plants such as honeysuckle and lavender can be monitored and used within mazes, play places, and special spaces as well. Maze projects will need to be started during the summer months to enjoy by the fall. Cornstalks can be planted in traditional rows for a "secret hideaway" feel.

Musical Refuge: Designate a play place to record sounds of nature—wind, rain, and birds, for example—in a cozy, out-of-the-way spot. Situate a canopy under a big tree to create the refuge. Hang netting or gauzy curtains for a gazebo effect. String leaves, bells, and flowers around the area. Place log stumps or crates inside for children to sit on. Fill a box or two with interesting instuments such as the following:

- an Autoharp
- a gourd rattle
- a small keyboard
- a child-sized guitar
- homemade coconut cymbals
- a variety of kazoos or "whizzers"
- recorders
- snake charmer's flute

- bamboo flutes

- an assortment of handbells

- small bongo drums

- old kitchen pots and pans

Additionally, offer a tape recorder with a microphone and headphones. Make a tape of nature sounds. Record a thunderstorm, windstorm, rainstorm, daytime birds chirping, nighttime crickets cheeping, or night owls *whoo*ing.

Nature Book Nook: Explore nature through an outdoor book nook. Include nature magazines, newspapers, puppets, flannel boards, paper, and writing utensils. Fill a crate or sturdy box with selected gardening books for children. Place accordingly in the area or near outdoor seating. Wonderful books include the following:

- *The Carrot Seed* by Ruth Krauss

- *Growing Vegetable Soup* by Lois Ehlert

- *Jack's Garden* by Henry Cole

- *Planting a Rainbow* by Lois Ehlert

- *Sunflower House* by Eve Bunting

- *The Ugly Vegetable*s by Grace Lin

Beautiful and realistic hand puppets are available through Wildforms: Gardening for Wildlife (www.wildforms.co.uk). Caterpillars, bats, red foxes, frogs, moles, snails, gray seals, badgers—even an owl with babies are available. Connect the puppets to stories in a nature book nook!

Gazebo Rain Shelter: A gazebo with screens is a perfect spot for outside story time and play. Hang teakettles and metal lids from the ceiling. Fill an old hope chest with a variety of picture books and textured blankets. Children can snuggle and read while in the shelter. If a gazebo isn't feasible, enlist the help of parents to position posts and set them in cement. Sheet metal can be secured over the top for a roof. Sheet metal is inexpensive, and it's wonderful for listening to the pitter-patter of rain on warm spring days. Hang wind chimes, bird feeders, or flowerpots from the ceiling.

Nature Spark

Allow natural music in the book nook. Make wind audible and visible by hanging colorful wind chimes, cowbells, and old metal teapots and watering cans. In *Natural Playscapes*, Rusty Keeler (2008) suggests painting old trash-can lids and situating them for children to jingle and jangle as they move about in the play place.

Enhance play places by adding a pair of binoculars, a birdbath, mini windmill, water fountain, bird feeder, birdhouse, wind chime, or wind sock. Children love to tote toys and materials; offer wagons, small wheelbarrows, and old fishing-tackle boxes (they will love the little individual compartments!). Plants enhance outdoor play places. Lock into all possible curriculum concepts using nature for play places.

Wide-Open Spaces or Slopes: Never underestimate the thrill of hills, slopes, dips, mounds, and open spaces. Take advantage of grassy vacant areas, uneven mounds, and slopes for ball games, running, and parachute play. Children enjoy rolling down hills on warm spring days or sledding on snowy ones in the winter. Bushes and shrubs provide secretive places. Build forts under spruce trees. Add and bury topsoil and slides directly into slopes. Open areas make games like chase, catch, leapfrog, and tag imaginative and physical. An open vacant lot with a tree is perfect for singing songs and strumming a banjo. Children can examine the weeds and flowers in open areas and vacant lots. *The Vacant Lot* by Dale Fife is a wonderful connecting story that will encourage children to study their surroundings closely. Read it to students prior to investigating empty areas.

Outdoor Seats, Stages, and Lofts

Bring excitement to outdoor play with creative seats, stages, and lofts for children to frolic and play in. Use a variety of items to create these spaces, including logs, boulders, and crates. PVC piping can muster a play stage entrance. Gardens and flower beds are perfect additions that children can incorporate into their play. Add easels to the stages or a beanbag toss game near the seating. Use a variety of imaginative props to set a beautiful stage for outdoor play.

Hay Bales: Set out hay bales for children to sit on. Depending on allergies and comfort, cover with blankets if needed.

Milk and Bread Crates: Plastic or old wooden milk and bread crates can be used as all types of furniture, including tables and chairs. They also act as great ends to hold up boards. Inverted into the ground, crates make wonderful stepping paths.

Boulders: Several large rocks can make seating for children during play. Boulders can also serve as mountaintops.

Benches: Simple child-sized benches are perfect for early child care settings. Visit www.bigtoys.com for bench possibilities and more.

Stumps and Logs: Tree stumps and logs make great play seating for the outdoors. Ask for a donation of one-quarter of a cord of firewood. Situate tree stumps and logs of different heights in the ground for stepping and balancing games, as shown in the following illustration:

FOR BALANCING AND STEPPING

FOR SITTING

Tires in Dirt: Tires partially buried in the dirt can make great seats and steps. Paint tires for added aesthetic appeal.

TIRES SITUATED INTO THE LANDSCAPE AS STEPS

Picnic Tables: Picnic tables are not necessarily just for sitting. They can serve as a dramatic play stage for activities, such as a sailing pirate adventure or a covered wagon on an open prairie adventure. Picnic tables can be used for picnics on warm winter days too.

Wood Platforms: Spare or donated plywood can be turned into a tap-dancing stage or dramatic-play loft. What about an airport tower with homemade spyglasses for watching incoming planes? Add an old stroller wheel for steering and flying planes and a variety of creative costumes and props to perform outdoor skits, musicals, and plays. Offer children a microphone or a karaoke machine. Please note: it is important that children not be constantly scraping the bottom of the barrel, so to speak, for outdoor play props. Keep them fresh and new!

Sectioned Sod: Plant mosaic patches of sod in the middle of dirt areas to act as a play stage. Fence in the grass with simple fencing or surround the area with rocks.

Cemented Tractor Tires or Cable Spools: A large tractor tire with the center filled to the top with cement can serve as a magical and magnificent stage for children (Tee 2004). A large cable spool securely situated on its side is another stage idea.

· ·

Closing Thoughts

Outdoor play is a vital part of a child's life. Special play places in nature can provide powerful learning opportunities for children. Using natural elements "allows children to develop many skills important to later learning and academic success" (Benson and Miller 2008, 28). Use nature as your guide to creatively implement early learning standards within each special outdoor play area. Lock into the up-close-and-personal view of the child's world to create your play places. Remember, it's those small, novel things that spark the biggest interest—a furry caterpillar on a flower or a small puddle left in the middle of the play yard after a spring rainfall. Do not forget that special play spaces will succeed if they lock into student interests; "offering open-ended materials in a variety of areas will spark children's imaginations and respond to their desire to continually rearrange and combine materials for exploration and invention" (Curtis and Carter 2005, 36).

Those who contemplate the beauty of the earth find reserves of strength that will endure as long as life lasts.

—Rachel Carson

Sensory-Integrated Nature Activities

You want to put more nature and wonder into your students' lives, right? Did you know that Rachel Carson (1956, 56), an eminent naturalist, advocated "preparing the soil" for children so they will desire knowledge of the natural world—and ultimately, knowledge of themselves in it. This chapter presents sensory-integrated nature activities for you to do just that!

Be sure to focus on challenging children within the activity or craft, and employ nature-oriented instructional strategies—learning approaches that specifically use nature to teach. Lace your curriculum with multimodal sensory learning opportunities and hands-on experiences, which support developmentally appropriate practice and help children thrive (Torquati and Barber 2005). Some of the nature-oriented instructional strategies you'll encounter in the activities include these:

- collecting items in nature
- labeling and displaying nature
- organizing and sorting nature specimens
- journaling in a nature journal or log
- observing changes in the weather
- performing nature experiments
- logging and charting data collected from nature

- using nature study tools such as microscopes, binoculars, and magnifying glasses

- sketching and painting things found in nature

- comparing and contrasting elements and items in nature

- reading books about nature

Given that multisensory learning is effective as a developmentally appropriate practice, incorporate as many or all of the senses as possible within the strategies and activities. In doing so, children will have an easier time learning and retaining the information you present to them.

· ·

Fifty-Eight Sensory-Integrated Nature Activities Laced with Nature-Oriented Instructional Strategies

Below are fifty-eight sensory-integrated nature activities that utilize nature-oriented instructional strategies. Use the exercises outside in the special play places, seats, stages, and lofts presented in chapter 3. The exercises can also be used in the classroom and while on field trips and hikes. In most cases, the activities are simple and do not call for a long list of supplies, and the appendix lists additional resources to get you over any hurdles. Be optimistic. As I tell my students, "The only difference between ordinary and *extraordinary* is a little 'extra.'" For example, toss-ins (see page 115) add flare to activities. Enjoy the activity options provided here:

Berry Bouncing: My grandmother taught me that fresh cranberries bounce! This is how she would test them for freshness when she made her delicious cranberry bread. She would hold a cranberry above her head and drop it. If it bounced, we washed it, sliced it, and tossed it in the mixing bowl. If it didn't bounce, we "bounced" it into the trash can. Have children do the "berry bounce." Put a twelve-inch piece of tape on the floor. Tape a small six-inch square directly in front of the tape line. Have the child put her toes behind the line. Hand the child a cranberry. Have her hold it directly in the air over the tape box and drop it, trying to hit inside the box. If the berry bounces, put it in the berry box. If not, toss it in the trash can. Enhance the activity by making cranberry bread in class. Let children help add the cranberries and stir the batter. Children explore many senses in this activity, including their sense of smell, touch, and taste.

Berry Painting: Gather berries in different sizes, shapes, and textures. Possibilities include blueberries, strawberries, raspberries, and cranberries. Wearing nonlatex gloves or using a potato masher, let students *smash* and *smoosh* the berries in a big bowl. In addition to feeling their texture differences, have students smell the differences as aromas are released. Do some berries smell stronger than others? Put the berries to a taste test. Taste testing is dependent on allergies, of course. Transfer the berry "paint" onto a palette; plastic plates work well. Paint on card stock with brushes and sponges.

Berry or Seed Sorting: The ability to observe and discuss similarities and differences among objects in nature can be accomplished with berry or seed sorting. Categorizing and comparing challenges children to ask questions and look for answers. Ask children to sort berries by characteristics, such as color, texture, or size. Use a variety of seeds, such as sunflower, pumpkin, and bird varieties. While examining berries and seeds, ask, "What is the same about your seeds?" or "What is different about your berries?" Such questions often spark the sorting and categorizing process.

Binoculars, Telescopes, Periscopes, and More: Identify and explain the uses of as many nature-study tools as possible with children. Suggestions include a pair of binoculars, telescope, compass, sundial, wind vane, rain gauge, periscope, microscope, or magnifying glass. Visit www.discoverthis.com for an interactive talking microscope. Allow students to experiment with and explore the tools at a classroom center or outdoors in a play place or special space. As you share and demonstrate each tool, remember that most come in low- and high-magnification varieties.

Bird Feeders: A bird-feeding station can be a welcoming addition to any outdoor play area. Let children use their imagination

Nature Spark

Exploring berries with young children can be a graphing delight. Similarities and differences in berry color, texture, and smell abound. Discuss the similarities and differences of berry bushes. Why do some bushes have berries and some do not? The following berries lend themselves well to comparisons: blackberries, blueberries, boysenberries, cranberries, gooseberries, huckleberries, raspberries, and strawberries.

Nature Spark

Discuss with students how seeds move and get planted elsewhere, and graph seed-moving similarities and differences. Some seeds, such as burrs, hook onto pants or socks and get a free ride to their new destination; others, such as dandelion seeds, float. Some seeds, such as "helicopters," twirl their way to a new location. Still other seeds, such as pine, glide from place to place. Ants and squirrels carry seeds off too (Hauser 1998). Another seed tidbit: the insides of hard seeds, such as bean or pumpkin, can be examined by soaking in water for a few hours. The water loosens their skin.

Nature Spark

Here's a basic bird pudding recipe. Mix 1 cup dried fruit, ¼ cup bacon bits, 2 cups lard, 1 cup bread crumbs, and ½ cup birdseed in a bowl. Heat 2 cups lard in a saucepan until it melts and comes to a slow boil. Mix the lard drippings with the dried fruit, bacon bits, bread crumbs, and birdseed and stir until well coated. Before the mixture cools, put it into bird-feeding containers. Hang or place them where you want to observe birds feeding.

to make a bird feeder out of a gourd, pinecone, craft sticks, or a clean empty milk jug. A bagel smeared in peanut butter (as always, be aware of allergies), rolled in birdseed, and hung from a tree is a simple bird feeder. Guide student bird-feeder ideas. Make specialty feeders for hummingbirds or woodpeckers. Have students research and log birds' special feeding needs in their nature journals. A hands-on bird-feeder project can be delightful to children, especially if they are able to make goopy bird pudding to place inside or smother around their creation. Place homemade bird feeders near classroom windows and observe local bird species up close. Have students chart the most frequent flyers, as well as study their behavior while feeding.

Bug Bingo: Turn lotto games into bug, or insect, bingo. Visit www .discoverthis.com for bingo cards that provide basic "bugology" facts. Make your own cards with interesting and simple insect tidbits written on the front. Here are four to get your wheels churning:

- Insects have a three-part body—the head, thorax, and abdomen.

- Insects hatch from eggs.

- Insects have six legs. (Spiders have eight.)

- Insects have compound eyes.

For a more sensory bingo experience, turn bug bingo into nature bingo by using actual objects from nature. Students must match a drawn item with its placeholder. Collect the following items to use as nature bingo placeholders. The card illustration on the next page may also be helpful in sparking bingo ideas.

feather	bone of some kind
acorn	fossil
wildflower	pinecone
rock	burr
leaf	cocoon
cattail	twig with a bud
pine needle	piece of straw
piece of charred wood	

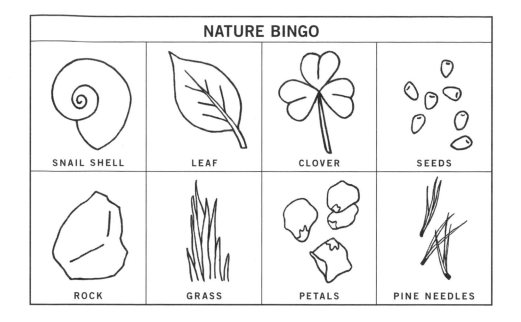

NATURE BINGO

| SNAIL SHELL | LEAF | CLOVER | SEEDS |
| ROCK | GRASS | PETALS | PINE NEEDLES |

Bug Houses: Upon seeing an odd-looking insect, children usually respond in one of three ways: Run from it! Stomp on it! Study it! (Korte, Fielden, and Agnew 2005). Bug houses are perfect for any reaction because they allow children to observe all kinds of creepy crawlies up close. Bug houses can be made out of simple materials, such as small plastic jars or clean, clear containers. Just insert holes into the lids for airflow.

Bug Hunt: Venture out on a bug hunt. You may hear "living" music—chirping crickets and buzzing bees. Use your homemade bug houses to store discoveries! Have students look for the creepy crawlers under logs, on trees, in bushes, and on the ground. Encourage lifting rocks, rustling through leaves, or digging dirt. Great bug-hunting kits consist of small hand lenses or pocket magnifiers, small aquarium nets, tweezers, baby food jars, jewelry boxes, and small notepads and pencils.

Build a Bug: Using natural clay, let children build a bug. Offer small twigs or pipe cleaners for insect legs, antennae, and other insect parts. Most early childhood curricula focus largely on butterflies or pill bugs when studying insects. Educators should allow children to observe a wide variety of insects, including tropical and exotic ones. Why not try Madagascar hissing cockroaches? They can be purchased from educational supply stores along with everything needed for their care, such as a cage, food, and instructions (Korte, Fielden, and Agnew 2005).

Nature Spark

Children will enjoy learning about lightning bugs, also known as fireflies. If you have lightning bugs in your region, catch several in a jar and let children take turns observing them in a closet or under a light blanket. Connect the activity to Eric Carle's beautifully illustrated book *The Very Lonely Firefly*.

Children will ooh and aah when able to scoop up floating nature and sunken treasure out of homemade canals, rivers, moats, runnels, and volcanoes. Make nets in various sizes and widths, as well as with different handle lengths. The variety will benefit children's fine-motor skills.

Butterfly or Bug Net: Making a small net to scoop up bugs, butterflies, and nature specimens is an easy nature project for children. Bug nets can hone a child's observation skills, as a variety of bugs, such as praying mantis and butterflies, are captured. Students can watch a snared praying mantis inch its way up their arm and swivel its head. Ask students if a butterfly would be as cooperative. To make a net you will need a small stick, branch, or bamboo pole. Bend a wire hanger into a circle, leaving a straight end for attaching the net to the stick. Tightly sew cheesecloth or mosquito netting around the wire hanger (Johnson 1997). This simple net will work well for catching bugs in flower or vegetable gardens where they are plentiful.

Characteristics of Nature: Have students sit outside and write observations in their nature journals. Offer a variety of sketching pens and pencils. Quill pens can be made from bird feathers and provide unique writing opportunities. Use thin paint as quill ink. Get students started by suggesting they sketch a blooming flower bud, moss-covered bark, or a hovering cloud.

Take a Collection: Leaves make a wonderful nature collection for young children because they come in many shapes, colors, and sizes. Use bags to collect all sorts of leaves according to the following criteria:

- shape—feather, hand-shaped, or oval

- texture—fuzzy or slick

- size—large, medium, or small

- autumn colors—yellow, red, brown, or orange

And don't forget to inform students that, regardless of a leaf's size, shape, or color, it does an amazing thing—it makes food for the tree (Hauser 1998).

If flowers from a natural setting are unavailable, call a local florist and ask for cuttings and trimmings. Let children take them apart to closely investigate petals and stems. Have students measure, sort, and graph a variety of donated flowers (Hachey and Butler 2009).

Dried Flowers: Dried flowers can be used for a variety of nature crafts. Use a heavy book to press flowers. Laminate flowers to make festive bookmarks, stationary, and cards. Use dried flowers in collages and to make potpourri, which can be used as a toss-in for mud-pie making. Place dried flowers under a sheet of paper and use chalk or colored pencils to make dried flower rubbings.

Earthquakes: To give children an earth-shaking earthquake experience, bring in a large comforter and have them take turns sitting in the middle of it. Instruct the other children to stand around the edge of the blanket and shake it back and forth, jiggling the blanket. Toss small balls in the middle for added sensory flare. This activity would make a great introductory activity to earthquakes.

"Fab Lab" Play: Outdoor "lab" work is especially wonderful after a rainstorm. The air and surroundings are fresh and vibrant in color and smell! Children can compare and contrast a variety of specimens—such as dirt, sand, and rainwater—in laboratory beakers. To make a "fab lab" that is enticing to children, set out lab coats, magnifying glasses, and goofy goggles. Fill plastic beakers full of vinegar, water, oil, and other odorous mixtures and homemade solutions. Dye beaker contents neon green, blue, and yellow.

When exploring nature, safety is a must. Introduce and explore safety in nature with an outside "fab lab." Here are several safety suggestions to enforce (Hirschfeld and White 1995):

- If you don't know what something is, do not touch it.

- Never put anything from an experiment or found in nature in your mouth.

- Make sure to wear protective goggles and gloves when working and exploring nature.

- Don't litter. Recycle and clean up within the environment as much as possible with students.

Gardening: Classrooms should incorporate a gardening project. Whether tending to small geraniums on a windowsill or a full-fledged outdoor vegetable patch, garden skills are invaluable. A wonderful resource for children's garden ideas is *Hollyhocks and Honeybees: Garden Projects for Young Children* by Sarah Starbuck, Marla Olthof, and Karen Midden. The appendix lists several other gardening resources.

Guest Speakers: Bring in guest speakers from area nurseries, farms, greenhouses, floral shops, pet stores, or other nature-related businesses and agencies. Invite university students studying biology, geology, or zoology to share their passions.

Nature Spark

A "fab lab" could open a door to the captivating world of chemistry. Embellish the possibility with creativity and a few good books full of chemistry ideas. Check out *Science Adventures: Nature Activities for Young Children* by Elizabeth A. Sherwood, Robert A. Williams, and Robert E. Rockwell and *Jump into Science: Active Learning for Preschool Children* by Rae Pica.

Nature Spark

Multiple-family garage sales, flea markets, and consignment stores are hot spots for dress-up clothes.

Nature Spark

To make an outdoor snack special, put it inside an ice cream cone; the cone acts as a cup. Cereal cone sundaes are a great outdoor treat. Let students scoop dry cereal, such as Kix, shredded wheat, or Chex (keep it healthy and not sugar-laden), as well as raisins, granola, pudding, shredded coconut, sliced fruit, and, of course, a dollop of whipped cream. Other outdoor treat ideas include the following:

- popsicles dipped in sprinkles
- cones filled with fresh berries
- seed trail mix using a variety of seeds, such as sunflower and pumpkin; toss in raisins

Enlist parents with interesting nature-oriented jobs to speak. Even nature experts, such as members of a community bird club, can be helpful resources (Ross 2000).

Inclement Weather Dress-Up: On especially snowy or rainy days, when students are trapped indoors, grant time to dress up in imaginative, weather-themed costumes. Don a costume yourself for the day; maybe a bright-colored floral apron and crown as *Ms. May Day*. Other ideas include *The Snow Fairy*, *The Rain Princess*, *Mr. March Wind*, or *Father Fog*. To accommodate the costumes, fill a large box with colorful raincoats, wigs, sunglasses, artificial flowers, and a variety of other imaginative props, such as homemade butterfly wings and an assortment of finger puppets. Read connecting stories to activate student imaginations. *The Paper Bag Princess* by Robert N. Munsch is a classic.

Ladybug Treats: Here is a yummy activity children can snack on while at an outdoor play center. Read Eric Carle's book *The Grouchy Ladybug*, and then create a yummy ladybug with students! The steps are simple:

1. Have students wash their hands.

2. Give each child half an apple. Have them remove the seeds.

3. Have students poke three holes on each side of their apple for ladybug legs. Insert small black licorice pieces in each hole.

4. Using peanut butter as paste (as always, be aware of allergies), have students glue raisins to the back of their ladybug for spots!

5. For the ladybug's head, use a grape or olive. Attach with a toothpick.

6. Enjoy the ladybug treat with students.

Here are more beautifully illustrated books by Eric Carle. Can you think of a snack idea to accompany each? Use rice cakes and sliced fruit and veggies to make storybook connections and treats for the following children's books.

- *The Mixed-Up Chameleon*

- *The Very Clumsy Click Beetle*

- *The Very Lonely Firefly*
- *The Very Hungry Caterpillar*
- *The Very Busy Spider*
- *The Foolish Tortoise*

Microscope Viewing: Set up a microscope-viewing area outdoors on a picnic table or within a play place. With students, view sugar grains, leaves, salt grains, newspaper, algae from a class pond project, sand grains—even dust bunnies collected from around the classroom.

Monet Painting: Introduce children to the beautiful landscapes and nature paintings of Claude Monet through prints and videos. Have children fingerpaint with boldly colored fingerpaints or softer pastels while standing at easels or picnic tables. *Baby Monet: Discovering the Seasons*, part of the Baby Einstein series, is a wonderful video for young children. It is a playful and vibrant introduction to Monet and to the sights and sounds of the seasons. Follow up with *Discover the Seasons* by Diane Iverson, a perfect book for teaching children ages three and up about winter, fall, spring, and summer.

Mud Masterpieces: What makes the best mud pies? Tell students that masterful mud pies don't crumble. They hold together like a hamburger patty. Let students explore mud and sand concoctions using a variety of materials to see which stuff makes the best mud pie. Let children experiment with oozy, gooey, gritty, and mushy mud textures by changing the amount of water and toss-ins in the mix. Have students add more sand than mud or more mud than sand. What happens? Mix in a handful of natural clay. What happens to the mixture then? Add dried leaves, grass clippings, or straw. Have students record their observations and findings in their nature journals to answer the question, "What makes the best mud pie?" (Hauser 1998).

Nature Collections: A nature collection can trigger curiosity, strengthen vocabulary, and signal environmental awareness for children. Collections of nature can awaken the senses in a variety of ways. For example, have students collect colorful fall leaves, wet leaves, spring leaves—even tree buds—to observe, organize, label, compare, and contrast their feel,

Nature Spark

When offering children painting activities, spice up paintbrush possibilities. Here are several creative suggestions:

- fingers
- dried corncobs
- feathers
- cotton
- ice cubes (insert a craft stick as a handle before freezing)
- pumpkin or watermelon rinds on a fork handle
- broccoli stems

Nature Spark

Early sensory-kinesthetic experiences, such as mudpie making, are wonderful for children. Hold an outdoor pie-making contest with students. Have them create an assortment of fresh mud pies, such as muddy pumpkin, "chocolate" cream, or sandy rhubarb. Make a chart of all the pie possibilities. Be sure to display an assortment of nature-oriented pie decorations, such as twigs, fine sand, and shells.

smell, and wonder! Display nature collections with creative mounting. Ice cube trays make great sorting trays. Nature collection possibilities include rock, twig, shell, butterfly, leaf, insect, wood, and seed. Seed collections can be extended to pods, cones, and parachutes, which are also known as helicopters. For more information on nature collections see *838 Ways to Amuse a Child* by June Johnson.

Nature Experiments: The possibilities available for performing simple nature experiments with children are endless. Investigate and grow mold or crystals. Create static with balloons rubbed on students' hair. Here's an especially simple one: Fill a clear plastic jar with rain- or pond water and let students observe how it changes. They will likely observe the growth of green algae and mosquito larvae (Satterlee and Cormons 2008). Cover the top of the jar with old pantyhose to keep the experiment contained, especially when growing bugs. Resources for nature experiments are in the appendix as well as online. Try http://tlc.howstuffworks.com/nature -experiments-for-kids.htm.

Nature Jewelry: Simple jewelry can be made from a variety of nature items, such as seeds, shells, or twigs strung on thick yarn. Natural clay can be shaped into small beads, pierced with a small hole, and then dried so they can be painted and strung as a bracelet. Bring in old sunglasses, small mirrors, and jewelry boxes to be decorated with small nature items. Good craft glue should do the trick for getting items to stick.

Nature Journal: Children best absorb nature activities when they are integrated across the curriculum, especially in reading and writing. A nature journal nurtures a child's sense of wonderment as well as his observation skills. Ask children to sketch or write in their nature journal. Teach them to record and organize information they have gathered from experiments and projects. Discuss how this information can be compared and contrasted, sequenced, sorted, and classified. Students can also paste relevant pictures or items, such as feathers and pods, into their nature journals.

Nature Matching: Take digital pictures of a variety of nature items. Show children the pictures and have them pair each picture

Nature Spark

Janice Pratt VanCleave's *Play and Find Out about Nature: Easy Experiments for Young Children* is a great resource full of more than fifty simple hands-on experiments inspired by questions from kids. Below are three sample questions:

- "Why does a dog pant?"
- "Why do peeled bananas turn brown?"
- "What is inside a seed?"

Nature Spark

Have even the youngest students use correct terminology when writing and labeling drawings in nature journals. This will help them better communicate their observations and strengthen their vocabulary. For example, if you are learning about bugs with hard shells, don't be leery of introducing terms such as *exoskeleton* or *molting*. Children know these are big words!

to its counterpart outside. Make some of the pictures easy to match, such as a recognizable tree the children pass by every day on their way outside. Make others less easy to match, such as a close-up shot of a blade of grass.

Natural Phenomena: Write the word *phenomena* on the board or post it somewhere in full view during circle time. Ask children how to pronounce the word. Ask them what they think it means. List and discuss a variety of natural phenomena, such as lightning, hurricanes, volcanoes, tornadoes, and earthquakes. What will hold children's interests here is the novel information about natural occurrences, especially if you present them with visuals and creative activities, such as movement with props. For example, have children twirl like a tornado with colored scarves. Avoid scaring students with abstract issues such as rain-forest destruction or global warming. Instead stay centered on defining what each is, where it most occurs, and why. Discuss the causes and effects of each. Explain that each is a natural occurrence. For example, here is a simple definition for earthquakes: an earthquake occurs when the ground shifts. Use your hands to demonstrate a back-and-forth shifting motion. Show the children California, a common earthquake spot, on a map. The phenomena words will build a richer vocabulary. Amazing slideshows are available online for children to explore the wonders of the natural world. Book resources are available as well, such as *Magic School Bus inside a Hurricane* by Joanna Cole. See the appendix for additional weather books.

Nature Mobiles: Need a simple and quick classroom decoration for parent-teacher conferences or open house? Turn student nature collections into insect mobiles. Display several around the classroom from a branch or clothes hanger using yarn. Have students select an insect from the list below and then research picture books to find as many facts as they can. String facts from the mobile. The mobile base would consist of a student-drawn picture of the bug. Insect mobile ideas include the following:

- ladybugs
- flies
- grasshoppers

- ants

- butterflies

- bees

- beetles

- roly-polies

- walking sticks

- crickets

- daddy longlegs

Nut Memory: Introduce children to the game "Nut Memory." Gather several nuts in their shells, such as walnuts, buckeyes, acorns, or Brazil nuts. Place one nut beneath each paper cup, and have players take turns selecting a pair of cups to see if they've found a matching set of nuts underneath. If a pair of matching nuts is discovered, the child keeps the pair of nuts and takes another turn. If not, a second player takes a turn (Hauser 1998). Always consider allergies when playing "Nut Memory."

Odds and Ends: Children enjoy sticking, twisting, and clumping things together. Using cones, seeds, pods, twigs, feathers, and other natural odds and ends, let them create wild animal sculptures. Use pipe cleaners, plastic-bag ties, masking tape, and craft glue to build fascinating odds-and-ends creations (Johnson 1997).

Petal Blowing: Gather a variety of flower petals—and pay attention to allergies with natural flower petals. Put down a long piece of tape on one end of a classroom table. Have children stand at the other end of the table and try to blow the petals past the finish line. Make it a two-child game, and see who can blow the most petals over the line. To enhance the game, let children use tweezers or chopsticks to pick up and sort the petal varieties in muffin tins or small cups. Feathers, cotton balls, or heavier items work as well as petals. Have the children blow through straws, plastic tubes, or noisy party blowers to push the petals along. Or use paint. Let children dip empty thread spools in paint and blow them onto paper through a bendy straw. Allow children to progress through the experience as independently as possible. This includes gathering nature items from outdoors to blow, chart, and write about in their nature journals after completing the activity.

Potato Eyes: Potatoes are actually the roots of a potato plant. They are often dirty when you buy them because they grow underground. A potato-eye experiment is simple. Bring in a variety of root vegetables, such as carrots, onions, and potatoes (sweet, red, and brown). Place each in an individual plastic bag. Set the bags in a corner and watch for "eyes" to grow. Ask students to draw what they see growing in their nature journals. Ask students why the eyes are growing.

Potpourri: Making potpourri is another fantastic sensory experience. Children explore the colors, textures, and fragrances of flowers. Have students pull the petals off a variety of flowers and place them in a small bowl. Ask a local florist for a donation of expired arrangements, if flowers are not readily available in your school setting. Let the flower petals dry for several days in a shallow dish, and then store in a sealed jar. Place homemade potpourri in a small bowl or wrap it in sachets.

Produce Exploration: Children will enjoy the ultimate sensory experience of exploring fresh vegetables and fruits with their hands. Children can shuck fresh corn or shell peas. Provide students with individual baskets or pots. Demonstrate the shucking and shelling process. Other supervised vegetable activities include grating carrots or peeling and mashing potatoes. Let children explore textures and smells of a variety of vegetables. Two additional vegetable exploration ideas include the following:

- Pry apart various fruits and vegetables to view seeds and feel the inside textures. Explore kiwis, papayas, cantaloupes, and bananas (red, purple, or yellow). Use fruits and vegetables that are ripe, overly ripe, or ready to eat. Compare and contrast the differences of each in nature journals.

- Allow students to pick and shell pea pods grown in a class garden project. Compare ripe and unripe peas. Ripe peas are robust in size and texture, whereas unripe peas are mushy and flat (Torquati and Barber 2005).

Nature Spark

When doing a potato-eye experiment be sure to introduce the word *auxin*. Have children define it in their nature journals. Auxin is a chemical that helps roots grow (Harris 2008, 27). A fine book to accompany potato-eye or root experiments is *One Potato: A Counting Book of Potato Prints* by Diane Pomeroy. If students grow potatoes in a class gardening project, bring in several slow cookers and bake potatoes as an afternoon treat. Put chives from a class garden project on top for flavor.

Pumpkin Goo: This is an awesome sensory experience. You'll need a pumpkin or two. Cut the tops off of them. With the children, scoop out the "goo" from inside the pumpkin. Let children play in the goo on cookie sheets or wax paper. Have them remove the seeds from the goo and sort, clean, and cook. Mud mixed with petroleum jelly is also great sensory goo that is irresistible to children!

Rain Band: Set up a rain band by placing hollow containers in a light rain shower. Turn coffee cans, aluminum pie plates, and plastic jugs upside down for the rain to fall on and produce pitter-pattering sounds. Cottage cheese containers or ice cream tubs with plastic wrap stretched over the top and filled with crispy rice cereal make a unique instrumental noise. Add other instruments, such as homemade kazoos, harmonicas, triangles, and flutes. Additional suggestions include the following:

- spoons: metal spoons of different sizes

- guitars: rubber bands strapped around a tissue box

- washboard: corrugated cardboard; strum it with a stick or spoon

- maracas: plastic soda bottles with rocks inside

- tambourines: paper plates stapled together with beans or rice inside

- drums: oatmeal boxes, big butter tubs with lids, coffee cans, empty paint cans, wooden or stainless steel bowls, or pots and pans

- megaphones: funnels and cardboard tubes

- cymbals: two metal pot lids, kettle lids, or pie tins

- gongs: toy mallets or wooden spoons to strike metal objects

- sand blocks: wooden blocks with sandpaper glued to them

- shakers: keys to jingle and jangle; plastic jars, milk jugs, paper bags, or butter tubs filled with rice (with the lids on tight)

Rainbow Making: A rainbow is most visible when the sun comes out right after a rain shower. You can make a rainbow with students using a garden hose. With your back to the sun, spray a fine mist in front of you. Ask students to observe the colors

Nature Spark

Use a variety of small items to create homemade instruments that produce an assortment of sounds. Use paper clips, washers, seeds, rice, beads, bolts, coins, cereal, beans, sugar, pebbles, marbles—even water. Play a sound guessing game. What's inside?

Nature Spark

Did you know Thomas Locker has three marvelous, award-winning nature books: *Water Dance*, *Mountain Dance*, and *Cloud Dance*? Beautifully illustrated, they are a "must" to add to your classroom library.

they see. Do they blend into one another? See if you can spray a *double* rainbow, two rainbows appearing at once (Hirschfeld and White 1995).

Rain Painting: Have students use the rain to paint a pretty picture. Using tempera paint, splotch several big paint patches on your paper. Take students outside and let them circle the playground once with their painting held out in front of them. Don't stay out too long or masterpieces will turn into soggy messes! Let children give their portrait a name—maybe *Rain Dance!* (Hauser 1998).

Rock Sort: Introduce children to the world of geology and the tools geologists use, such as rock hammers and waterproof paper. Have children gather an assortment of rocks to sort and classify. With students, establish how rocks can be sorted according to hardness, color, texture, or size. Line up rocks from biggest to smallest, heaviest to lightest, darkest to lightest, or smoothest to roughest. Turn rocks into a mounted and labeled collection.

Scarecrow: During the fall season, build a crafty-looking scarecrow with children. It will make a wonderful addition to a class garden or play place full of flowers and veggies. Send a newsletter home beforehand asking for scarecrow-clothing donations, such as plaid shirts, old work boots, jeans, gloves, belts, vests, straw hats, and suspenders. Use a pillowcase stuffed with straw as a head. Sew on button eyes or draw the face with permanent markers. For the scarecrow's body, use a basic wooden stake in the shape of a cross. Use safety pins to secure clothing. Let your imagination do the rest. For a fast "family" scarecrow display, use upside-down straw brooms with large brown paper bags over the top. Have students draw faces on the bags. Add colorful yarn hair to each scarecrow family member. Give each a straw hat or big bonnet. Let children name the scarecrow people and write about their adventures in their nature journal.

Seed Sponges: The class that gardens together learns together. This nature activity makes a great gift. Cut a variety of sponges into various shapes, such as a circle, heart, or star. Soak the sponge shape in water, then wring out. The sponge

Nature Spark

Rocks are abundant in nature and yield countless activities. Rocks can be dipped in paint, weighed on scales, or used as hopscotch markers. Explore rocks through magnifying lenses. Do comparison activities using quartz, slate, pumice, sandstone, limestone, or marble. Encourage children to start a rock collection when they visit places such as relatives' homes in other states or regions. And don't forget to turn over rocks—some of the neatest things can be found under them!

Nature Spark

Giving children the opportunity to grow their own plant from seeds will not only send a positive message about the natural world, but also nurture an assortment of science skills. Use a variety of seeds, such as lima beans, sweet potatoes, and avocados. Bean soup mixes have an assortment of seeds for children to sort and sprout. Be sure to share the responsibility of plant care with children; you facilitate the watering and growth process.

Nature Spark

Giant tomato sauce or chili cans make great containers for comparing sink or float items in water. Make sure to tape down any sharp edges with duct tape.

Nature Spark

After a heavy snowfall, go outside and let students toss handfuls of nuts in their shells. Then come back later to see what happened to them. Children will marvel at the empty shells scattered about, evidence that a squirrel or other animal discovered the winter treat.

should be wet but not dripping wet! Place the soggy sponge on a plate and sprinkle with seeds. Cover the dish with plastic wrap at night and leave unwrapped during the day. Give the sponge plenty of sunlight. Keep the sponge wet by misting it down with a water bottle (Hirschfeld and White 1995). Seeds should sprout in about twelve days. Let children chart their seed progress and then give the green shape as a gift. For increased sensory value, germinate bean, radish, corn, or squash seeds in moist paper towels. Allow students to dissect, examine, and compare and contrast the insides of the sprouting seeds. Lettuce leaves can be sown in the holes of moist sponges as well.

Shell Boats: Children enjoy sailing tiny boats. Use half a walnut shell or a split peach pit to create a boat. Place a small blob of clay or mud in the halved shell. Push a small twig with a paper triangle inserted through the top as a sail. Use shell boats to sail in class pond projects or on outdoor water tables. Cups, Styrofoam, tinfoil, corks, and pieces of sponge make great boats, as well as creative avenues to explore buoyancy.

Sink or Float: Set out a variety of small nature items, such as a pebble, cork, lump of clay, pinecone, leaf, rock, flower petal, and small twig. Have children drop each item in a medium bowl of water to predict if the item will sink or float. Use student nature journals to chart their discoveries. Share predictions and findings during circle time. If the weather is agreeable, use "sink and float" at an outdoor learning center.

Snow Candy: After a fresh and abundant snowfall, make old-fashioned molasses snow candy with students. Have students scoop up fresh snow and place it in several large pans. Pour premade hot sugar and molasses syrup, prepared on a Bunsen burner or hot plate together in class, into the pans over the snow. (A variety of simple molasses candy recipes are available online.) The syrup will harden once it hits the snow! Students will marvel at the reaction. Explain it to them: as the sugar and molasses are heated, the two dissolve together, or caramelize, making a sweet liquid. When the liquid is poured over the snow, it cools at an extreme rate and solidifies (crystallizes) over the shape and forms candy. The reaction is actually a phase change from a liquid to a solid! Add the new word *caramelize* to students' nature journals.

Snow Painting: Fresh blankets of snow make a perfect painter's canvas. Hit after-holiday sales for washable dyes children can use in the snow to create artwork. Students can paint snow sculptures or write in the snow with spray, squirt, and mist bottles full of colored water. See pages 70–71 for additional snow ideas.

Sticky Gloves: Turn old gardening gloves into sticky gloves! Wrap duct tape, stickyside out, around a pair of gloves. Sticky gloves are great for catching bugs and inspecting bark, fall foliage, flowers, weeds, and lichens on trees. It is a cinch to make them!

Thermometer Reading: Teach students to read a thermometer. Hang several thermometers outdoors and chart changing weather temperatures and patterns. Have students use their nature journals to record their observations.

Tornado Tubes: Allow children to become familiar with the mesmerizing and swirling life of a tornado vortex by having them make tornado tubes, otherwise known as "a tornado in a bottle." The experiment will stimulate problem-solving and observational skills, as well as trial-and-error situations. Venture online for simple tornado tube instructions.

Tree Watching: A simple observation project for students is to monitor a tree for a week or month. Here are several suggestions for purposeful tree watching. Have students answer and log the following questions in their nature journals:

- Where is the tree located? Draw it and its surroundings.

- How many branches does it have? Can you find any nests or critters (birds, squirrels) on its branches?

- Does the tree have leaves, lichen, fruit, or flowers? (The answer may depend on the season.)

- What do you notice about the tree's bark? What insects can you find?

Come up with additional questions or prompts for tree watching. You could even expand it over the year and have students draw their tree in the fall, winter, spring, and right before they leave for summer vacation (Hammerman, Hammerman, and Hammerman 2001).

Nature Spark

Snowflakes are amazing—one of nature's true masterpieces. Children can gain an understanding of their magnificence by viewing them through a magnifying glass while outdoors. After observing, go back inside and have students draw several in their nature journal or write a poem about snowflakes.

Nature Spark

Take students on a tree safari to study school-yard trees. Discuss how trees provide shade, homes for animals, oxygen for people and plants to breathe, and wood to make things. Look for oak, apple, cherry, pine, walnut, cedar, spruce, orange, or pecan trees (depending on region). A wonderful tree story to connect to their outing is *The Man Who Planted Trees* by Jean Giono. Additional safari ideas include the following:

- Find a tree that has buds on it.
- Find a tree with a nest in it.
- Watch a tree in the wind.
- Find a tree in the shade.
- Find a young tree in the school yard.
- Find an old tree in the school yard.
- Watch a tree in the rain.

Water Forms: Teach children that water comes in three different forms—a liquid you can pour, a solid like an ice cube, or a gas steaming from a hot teakettle. Water can also change from one form to another. Let children experiment with this concept. Place a small paper cup full of water in the freezer. Once frozen, remove and let students watch it melt back into a liquid (Hirschfeld and White 1995). Bring in a hot plate and a teakettle. Safely observe steam with students. Comment on, discuss, and compare the similarities and differences of water forms in their nature journals.

Water Soak: An outdoor water-soak center is an ideal activity for a warm spring afternoon. At a picnic table, display a variety of materials, such as foil, waxed paper, a handful of cotton balls, leather, a sponge, a rock, newspaper, a wad of paper towels, and a piece of wood. Ask students which of the materials would make a good raincoat. Which would not? Set out several turkey basters and eyedroppers along with several bowls of water for students to test the materials. Log the results on a large graph or in their nature journals.

Weather Chart: Seasonal weather changes present children with firsthand learning and play opportunities. Add a simple weather prediction chart to morning circle time. Introduce a meteorologist's job and let children take turns forecasting the weather with a microphone. Use a variety of weather words for students to read and chart each day. Let students make a symbol to represent each weather prediction. A weather chart will not only enhance their vocabulary, but also teach children a variety of ways to describe and observe nature. Use the weather word chart on the next page for creative weather-data predicting and recording ideas. Please note: several of the words, such as *breezy*, *gusty*, and *windy*, are very similar in meaning but encourage vocabulary expansion. Discuss their subtle differences.

After children have mastered the weather word chart, add weather phrases, such as "cloudy with a chance of rain" or "a sunny fall day." A wonderful weather-related read for this activity is *Weather Words and What They Mean* by Gail Gibbons.

Nature Spark

Listen to *The Four Seasons* by Antonio Vivaldi with the children. The musical composition denotes each season of the year. See if children can guess each season as they listen to the piece. Great books on the seasons and weather include *Seasons on the Farm* by Jane Miller and *The Year at Maple Hill Farm* by Alice and Martin Provensen. Another simple idea: children can draw and write observations about the current season in their nature journals. Take them outdoors to look for signs of the season. Prompt their drawings with questions, such as "What season is it?" or "When does the sun set during this season?" or "Do flowers bloom during this season?" (Crawford et al. 2009).

THE WEATHER TODAY IS _____.				
(Let students fill in the blank and attach a symbol.)				
breezy	gusty	bright	clear	cloudy
damp	drizzling	dry	foggy	hailing
thundering	lightning	rainy	sleeting	misting
sprinkling	sunny	wet	windy	snowy

Weed Bouquets: A simple nature gift is a weed bouquet. Let children pick dried weeds and dandelions for a specially arranged weed bouquet. Make a vase to take home to mom with an accompanying card. For the card, glue dry seeds and spare weeds onto paper. Create a variety of table and wall arrangements using leftover dried weeds and seeds.

Who Was . . . ? Introduce students to famous naturalists and their work through books, interactive field trips, museum exhibits, technology, photographs, and paintings. Well-known naturalists include the following:

- Rachel Carson—nature writer and marine biologist
- John Muir—father of our national parks
- Dian Fossey—zoologist who studied gorillas

Wildlife Collages: Use old nature magazines and nature pictures of local wildlife to make collages. Supply a variety of cutting utensils, such as scissors with different-shaped edges. Collages can be made out of natural specimens, such as leaves, dried flowers, and pods. Heavy paper, such as card stock, is recommended for nature collages.

Windsock Art: Bring wind to life by having students make a simple windsock! Start off with a large piece of colorful fabric for the base. Use newspaper, magazine, or brown-paper-bag strips that have been reinforced with card stock. These are the ends that flap in the wind. Hang the windsock outside near a window. Have students chart wind observations each day by watching their sock. Is it a mildly windy day? Very windy? Use a windsock as a small prompt for a weather chart.

Nature Spark

Wind can be made audible and visible with the use of various wind toys, such as pinwheels, toy sailboats, parachutes, wind vanes, wind chimes, waving wind wands, rippling ribbons, fluttering flags, and traditional kites. Have a windy day party!

Zoo and Museum Visits: A visit to a local zoo or museum provides children opportunities to explore nature, science, math, and art concepts (Henderson and Atencio 2007). Museum and zoo visits should be an integral part of teaching to bring out a child's inner nature lover. It is important that educators be organized and intertwine curriculum objectives. Teachers should ask the following questions prior to a museum or zoo visit (Henderson and Atencio 2007):

- Can information about the museum or zoo be sent to me before the visit? What are the rules of the museum or zoo? No touching or hands-on?

- What areas of the museum are age appropriate for my students?

- Is there a place for children to break for lunch?

- Will a staff member guide the visit?

- Do children need to be arranged in groups for interactive or behavioral purposes?

- How will students be paired? (Learning buddies are effective for museum and zoo visits.)

- Will students be grouped to tour the exhibits?

- Will the trip require chaperones? If so, how many?

- Will any preparatory lessons need to be incorporated into the curriculum prior to the trip?

- Do I need to establish any new behavior rules?

Nature Music, Rhymes, Riddles, and Tongue Twisters

Research and theory supports the creative use of music in early childhood education. Music is one of the most direct avenues to critical thinking because it requires neither words nor symbols to be perceived. A child's self-confidence is boosted when she is invited to sing, move, or play in a musical group. According to Howard Gardner, the musical learning intelligence is the earliest to surface and plays a significant role in a child's intrinsic development (Cornett 2003). In addition, research suggests that exposure to music can enhance young children's cognitive development (Snyder 1997). Give children musical activities that incorporate nature songs with a creative use of phonetic sounds and letters. Look at several lines from "Willoughby Wallaby Woo":

> Willoughby Wallaby Woo,
> An elephant sat on you.
> Willoughby Wallaby Wee,
> An elephant sat on me!

Do you see how mesmerizing this song could become to children when embellished with robust nature props and large percussion or homemade instruments? The following are possibilities:

- Make harmonicas with children by folding a piece of tissue paper over the teeth of a comb. Hum through the paper to create the sound.

- Make a set of cymbals with two metal pot covers. Tie a long piece of yarn around each handle. Strike the pot covers together for playful sounds.

- Make a guitar with an empty shoe box and rubber bands. Stretch the rubber bands around the shoe box. The lid can be on or off. Leave the lid on for more durability. To play, strum the rubber bands.

Regardless of genre or sound, music is an essential part of a complete educational experience. Here are some rhymes and songs that will boost outdoor nature interactions, as well as provide abstract and concrete classroom experiences.

Musical Rhymes and Songs

Children construct an understanding of the world around them when offered children's books, music, rhymes, and other imaginative resources (Zeece 1999). Language skills can be developed through musical experiences that promote the naming and labeling of objects, actions, and people—or animals portrayed as people in playful ways (Zeece 1999). Such can be accomplished with the use of nature-oriented music, rhymes, riddles—even tongue twisters.

Nature Spark

Music has a powerful influence on children! Chants and nursery rhymes help children improve reading, memorization, and comprehension skills. Plus, the rhythmic patterns of chants and rhymes help children practice the language skills of accenting and syllabication (Hill-Clarke and Robinson 2004). Combined with nature, music in and out of the classroom is so much more than do-re-mi!

I'M A LITTLE ACORN BROWN

Use the rhyme as a way to introduce a seed-sorting or collection activity. Ask children where acorns are found. What animal eats them? Why do they have holes in them? Collect a jarful for children to observe and use with other craft activities. Do a variety of hand and foot movements with this short musical rhyme. Get especially creative with the last verse, "I'm a nut, I'm a nut!" Have children march to it waving their arms in the air.

> I'm a little acorn brown
> Living on the cold, cold ground.
> Everybody steps on me.
> That is why I'm cracked, you see.
> I'm a nut. (clap, clap)
> I'm a nut. (clap, clap)
> I'm a nut, I'm a nut, I'm a nut.

Nature Spark

Incorporate creative movement into songs and rhymes. Ask children to move and make noises like the animals of "Old Macdonald Had a Farm." Present challenges about animals and their shape or sounds, such as "Show me how you can be round like a pig" or "Can you move like a rooster?" Creative movement activities foster imagination, problem solving, and self-expression (Pica 2009).

OLD MACDONALD HAD A FARM

This is a traditional children's favorite. Farm life is full of nature lessons and connections. Use the song to introduce a farm unit or a trip to a farm, and add alternate animal sounds. Once again, be creative.

> Old Macdonald had a farm, E-I-E-I-O.
> And on his farm he had some chicks, E-I-E-I-O.
> With a chick, chick here, and a chick, chick there,
> Here a chick, there a chick,
> Everywhere a chick, chick.
> Old Macdonald had a farm, E-I-E-I-O.

THERE WAS AN OLD LADY WHO SWALLOWED A FLY

This rhyming and sequencing song is wonderful for young children, and it is available in several storybook forms as well, including *There Was a Cold Lady Who Swallowed Some Snow* by Lucille Colandro—perfect to culminate outside snow activities. Other renditions include the following:

- *There Was an Old Lady Who Swallowed a Trout*

- *There Was an Old Lady Who Swallowed a Bat*

- *There Was an Old Lady Who Swallowed a Shell*

You can also try a pond, woodland, or rain-forest rendition. Have children come up with the food chain.

The original verses are as follows:

There was an old lady who swallowed a fly.
I don't know why she swallowed a fly—perhaps she'll die!
There was an old lady who swallowed a spider
That wriggled and wiggled and tickled inside her.
She swallowed the spider to catch the fly.
I don't know why she swallowed a fly—perhaps she'll die!

Add on several size-sequencing animal lyrics, including a bird, cat, dog, cow, and, of course, a horse!

FUZZY WUZZY

"Fuzzy Wuzzy" is fun! Add creative movements, such as walking on all fours like a bear. Chant the rhyme in a gruff Papa Bear voice or a quiet Baby Bear voice. Ask students if they think Mama Bear was a fuzzy-wuzzy bear and wore fuzzy-wuzzy slippers. Read *Goldilocks and the Three Bears* during circle time to extend the idea.

Fuzzy Wuzzy was a bear,
Fuzzy Wuzzy had no hair.
When Fuzzy Wuzzy lost his hair,
He wasn't very fuzzy,
Was he?

THE EENSY WEENSY SPIDER

This is another classic hand movement rhyme to use when introducing or studying spiders. Substitute other rhyming words for *waterspout*. A reinvented line might sound like this: "The eensy-weensy spider crawled up the long grapevine. Down came the rain and washed the spider out of line." Get goofy. Add to the experience by collecting insects and spiders in a jar for children to observe their movement. Let students free the critters afterward. Substitute a cricket or ant into the rhyme for a change-up. For peculiar information on crickets, ants, spiders, and other small creatures, see *Adventuring in Nature* by Betty Price.

The eensy-weensy spider crawled up the waterspout.
Down came the rain and washed the spider out.
Out came the sun and dried up all the rain,
And the eensy-weensy spider climbed up the spout again.

Nature Spark

Use nature-oriented music, rhymes, riddles, and tongue twisters to welcome children to circle time or story time; create a calm, relaxing mood as children clean up or transition from one activity to another; settle children for naptime; and refocus children when the atmosphere gets out of control (Shore and Strasser 2006).

Nature Spark

Here are several interesting bear facts to share with students. Male bears are *boars*; female bears are *sows*; young bears are *cubs*. A group of bears is called a *pack* or *sloth*. Another bear song to sing when studying the woods or berries is *The Bear Went over the Mountain*.

Nature Spark

Did you know that spiderwebs are actually sparkling strands of silk? To let students view a beautifully woven spiderweb, hold a flashlight underneath the web. Discuss what is viewed.

BABY BUMBLEBEE

This simple rhyme can generate a wide variety of activities and crafts. Children can explore, compare, and contrast wasps, hornets, and bumblebees.

> I'm bringing home my baby bumblebee.
> Won't my mommy be so proud of me?
> I'm bringing home a baby bumblebee.
> Ouch! It stung me!

Children like to really ham up the "Ouch!" Come up with several actions for it, such as jumping into the air or falling to the ground. A storybook with realistic bumblebee illustrations includes *In the Trees, Honeybees* by Lori Mortensen.

THE ANTS GO MARCHING

This summertime favorite can be accompanied with a variety of hand and feet movements, not necessarily a march. Let children observe an ant colony with binoculars. Discuss the strength of ants and other amazing tidbits, such as the following:

- Ants can carry many times their own weight.

- Ants work together to carry heavy pieces of food back to their colony.

- If a piece of food is too heavy, an ant will try dragging it while walking backwards.

- If it is still too heavy, an ant will tear it up into small pieces and carry it one small piece at a time.

> The ants go marching one by one, hurrah, hurrah.
> The ants go marching one by one, hurrah, hurrah.
> The ants go marching one by one,
> The little one stops to suck his thumb,
> And they all go marching down
> Into the ground
> To get out of the rain.
> Boom. Boom. Boom!

IT'S RAINING, IT'S POURING

"It's Raining, It's Pouring" is a simple tune that introduces or culminates any rainy day nature activity. See pages 68–69 for several suggestions.

Nature Spark

Call a local high school science department and request spare or sample bug collections to display in your early childhood classroom. Many high school students have to put a collection together. All it takes is a phone call.

It's raining, it's pouring,
The old man is snoring.
He went to bed and bumped his head
And couldn't get up in the morning.

THE RAINDROP SONG

Another rainy day tune is "The Raindrop Song." (Sing it to the tune of "Three Blind Mice.") It is perfect for connecting to a rain unit that teaches children how rain helps to water plants and keeps them from dying. Tie the song to making a rain gauge. Use a tall glass jar with straight sides. Mark the sides of the jar in quarter-inch intervals. Place the gauge in an open outdoor area near your classroom. Note the amount of rain after the next rainfall.

Three raindrops (hold up three fingers),
Three raindrops.
See how they fall (make fingers fall like raindrops),
See how they fall.
They all fall down from the clouds in the sky;
They water the plants so they won't die;
The plants feed the animals who live nearby;
Three raindrops.

THREE GREEN SPECKLED FROGS

Although originally a poem, this catchy rhyme can be turned into a musical jingle. Add hand and body movements for a quick rhythmic version. Repeat with two frogs and then one and so forth. The last verse is: "Then there were no more speckled frogs."

Three green speckled frogs
Sat on a speckled log
Eating some most delicious bugs.
YUM YUM!
One jumped into the pool
Where it was nice and cool.
Then there were two green speckled frogs.

TINY TIM

"Tiny Tim" is an imaginative yet simple tune. Children love it! Strum a guitar as the children sing and pretend to swim on the floor or hold a tiny turtle in cupped hands.

Nature Spark

To celebrate the outdoors with music, movements, and imagination, check out *Nature Notes for Little Folks,* a delightful CD for children to explore natural musical symphonies while outdoors. Visit www.redleafpress.org for details.

Nature Spark

Play nature music in the background during classroom or outdoor activities. As Martha Giles (1991, 44) confirms, "Most kids function very well with music in the background, and the right music at the right time can make them less stressed, more relaxed, happier, and more productive."

Balloon maracas are simple instruments for children to make. Put some rice in a balloon and blow it up. Use a variety of items, such as salt, split peas, or small beads to fill the maracas. Have children compare their sounds. Balloons can be turned into drums. Let children thump on their balloon with a soda straw.

I had a little turtle.
His name was Tiny Tim.
I put him in the bathtub
To see if he could swim.
He drank up all the water;
He ate up all the soap.
And now he's sick in bed
With a bubble in his throat.
Bubble, bubble, bubble, bubble,
POP!

On the last line—"POP!"—have children stand, jump, and clap their hands. This preschool classic makes a wonderful accompaniment to bubble play.

Riddles and Tongue Twisters

Children crave silly riddles and tongue twisters! Learning to recite riddles and rhymes is important for young children because doing so aids in reading mastery. Add simple nature-oriented riddles and tongue twisters to circle time or story time for children. The laughter that sparks will stimulate the brain and increase learning and retention potential (Silberg 2004).

Here are several amusing riddles and tongue twisters to use anytime. Some of the riddles are familiar. You may have heard them while growing up. Others have been adapted from *101 Nutty Nature Jokes* by Melvin Berger. Share them with students. Add as many descriptive words to them as possible, which makes for excellent imagery practice for children.

RIDDLES

Q: What kind of big and fast animal do you never play with?
A: A Cheat-tah!

Q: What happened when the crazy scientist with big green
    glasses put big sticks of dynamite in his fridge?
A: It blew its cool!

Q: Why did the funny farmer plant his big brown potatoes in bags?
A: So they wouldn't get dirt in their eyes!

Q: Why did the King Lion spit out the little clown?
A: Because he tasted funny.

Q: What did the mama firefly say to her son?
A: "You are so bright!"

Q: What did the banana do when it saw the big brown bear?
A: It split!

Q: What kind of colorful bow cannot be tied?
A: A rainbow.

Q: How do you repair a broken pumpkin?
A: With a pumpkin patch!

Q: Why don't pigs get sunburns?
A: Because they wear suntan "oink"-ment!

Q: What is a fuzzy gray mouse's favorite game?
A: Hide-and-squeak.

Q: Why do birds fly south for the winter?
A: They can't drive.

Q: What did the papa earthworm say to his daughter?
A: "Where on earth have you been?"

Q: What did the owl say to his best friend?
A: "I sure do give a hoot about you!"

Q: How do you call a frog?
A: You call the *hoperator*.

Q: Which flowers give the best kisses?
A: Tulips.

Q: Which tree can clap?
A: The palm!

Q: What color is the wind?
A: Blew.

Q: What are a bird's favorite cookies?
A: Chocolate *chirp*.

Q: Why did the fish cross the ocean?
A: To get to the other tide.

Q: What did the monkey say when his sister had a baby?
A: "I'll be a monkey's uncle!"

Nature Spark

Share with students that potato plants initially begin as flowers but do not generate seeds. A potato plant reproduces through its "eye"—a root growing off of the potato (Harris 2008). Set up an eye-producing potato experiment with students. See page 99 for experiment details.

Nature Spark

Did you know that the first jack-o'-lanterns were made out of turnips? But then someone finally figured out it was easier to carve a pumpkin than a turnip. Two wonderful pumpkin stories include *Pumpkin Pumpkin* by Jeanne Titherington and *The Tiny Seed* by Eric Carle.

TONGUE TWISTERS

A scary skunk sat on a small stump.
The skunk thumped the stump,
And the stump stunk from the skunk's thump.

Goosey geese graze in the golden green grass.

How much wood would a woodchuck chuck if a woodchuck could
    chuck wood?
He would chuck, he would, as much as he could,
And chuck as much wood as a woodchuck would
If a woodchuck could chuck wood.

Peter Piper picked a peck of pickled peppers.
A peck of pickled peppers Peter Piper picked.
If Peter Piper picked a peck of pickled peppers,
Where's the peck of pickled peppers Peter Piper picked?

Zebras zig and zebras zag.
Zebras zip and zebras zap as they zig their zag.

Black bug bit a big black bear, but where is the big black bear that
    the big black bug bit?

A big bug bit the bossy beetle before the bossy beetle bit the big
    bug back.

Sarah sells seashells on the seashore so she can sell seven more.

. . . .

Muck, Mud, and More

Materials like natural clay, sand, and mud are fabulous natural
substances for children to explore and get messy with. They
stimulate the senses and give students a chance to experience a
variety of smells and textures, as well as to develop fine-motor
skills. Natural substances, made extra mucky and messy, allow
children to let loose with their imagination and creativity. Use
the following natural substances to entice children in outdoor
play places, special spaces, and classroom learning centers.

Toss-Ins

Below is a chart of toss-ins—herbs, spices, scraps, and baubles that add flare to mud pies, water tables, and more. Accessories such as rolling pins, cookie cutters, funnels, melon scoopers, pastry tubes, plastic knives, pizza cutters, potato mashers, dough extruders, and proper storage containers are also handy when working with nature muck and more.

FOODS	CRAFTS	NATURAL ELEMENTS	HERBS/ EXTRACTS
oatmeal	sequins	evergreen needles	basil
coffee grounds	yarn scraps	dried leaves	nutmeg
crushed eggshells	glitter	flower petals	vanilla
gelatin mixes	lace bits	sand	peppermint

Mud Muck

Materials: 2 cups mud, 2 cups sand, ¼ cup dried rice, ½ cup salt, 1 teaspoon flavored extract, and water

Slowly add ingredients until the mixture is a desired consistency. Add cornstarch to thicken if needed.

Sawdust Stuff

Materials: 2 cups laundry detergent, 2 cups sawdust, water, and food coloring

Slowly add ingredients until at a desired consistency. Add cornstarch to thicken if needed.

Gunk

Materials: 2 cups salt, ½ cup oatmeal, ½ cup cornstarch, and ⅔ cup water

Mix salt and water in a big bowl. Heat for three to four minutes. Remove and add cornstarch, oatmeal, and ½ cup water. Stir briskly until desired consistency is achieved.

Ooey Stew

Materials: cornstarch, water, food coloring, and toss-ins

Mix ingredients in a large mixing bowl to desired consistency. Use cornstarch to control the texture. I suggest rotating the texture focus of the stew. Make it extra sticky one day and more

Nature Spark

Children can paint outdoors with simple fingerpaint mixtures, such as soap flakes mixed with a variety of toss-ins until a desired consistency is reached. Other ideas include shaving cream mixed with food coloring and natural toss-ins, such as seeds; tempera paint mixed with craft glue, washed sand, crumbled leaves, and pebbles; baby oil mixed with nature specimens. In addition to brushes, apply paint with sponges, wheat stalks, feathers, empty roll-on deodorant bottles, cotton balls, spools, celery stalks, potato halves, dry corncobs, halved bell peppers, wads of fabric, pinecones, and rubber stoppers.

pourable the next. Add toss-ins, such as tiny yarn scraps, crumbled dried flowers, lace bits, or colored salt and sand. Add bowls, cups, spoons, ladles, and measuring utensils for proper stew play.

Sand Paint

Materials: 1½ cups dry sand and 3 tablespoons paint (tempera works best)

Mix ingredients together to desired consistency. For thicker paint, add more sand. For thinner paint, add more paint.

Supersized Outdoor Bubbles

Materials: 2 cups water, 4 tsp. liquid dish soap, ½ tsp. sugar, 1 tsp. glycerin

Mix ingredients and use outdoors as soon as possible. Offer a variety of bubble wands.

Closing Thoughts

Learning for young children should not be confined to classroom walls. Knowledge gained through the use of nature-oriented activities is retained far longer than if simply read (Hammerman, Hammerman, and Hammerman 2001). Children who have the opportunity to be connected firsthand to nature usually learn more quickly. The beauty of an outdoor "living" laboratory is that children can dive into intensive investigation without the usual school-day interruptions (Hammerman, Hammerman, and Hammerman 2001). By implementing a wide variety of sensory-integrated nature activities and instructional strategies, teachers allow children the opportunity to explore the curriculum in extraordinary ways. Adding simple nature songs, riddles, rhymes, and tongue twisters ignites student interests and will pay off in academic dividends.

Appendix

As an early childhood instructor at a community college, one of my most overwhelming tasks is selecting quality children's literature, software, and additional curriculum resources to recommend to my students. I refer to the task as overwhelming, because every year the selection not only becomes more abundant in quantity, but also in quality! For me, looking for resources is like being a kid in a candy store; making a final top ten wish list is a true challenge.

Regardless of genre, children's books enhance a nature-driven curriculum. Literature can set the stage for nature exploration and wonderment. When a child reads a book of interest and then connects the concept to the outdoors, learning and wonderment are primed. Effective early childhood professionals realize that using developmentally appropriate literature, software, and other resources to enhance and complement the curriculum is important. Every book, CD, video, computer game, or kit has the potential to be a child's individual workshop of wonder.

In this appendix, you will find books, journal articles, software, educational kits, videos, DVDs, and other resources to complement the four previous chapters. Multidiscipline,

Genres of early childhood literature are numerous. How many do you make available to students? For ongoing inspiration and support in implementing nature into the curriculum, I recommend using a variety of the genres listed.

- informational or nonfiction books
- traditional tales and stories
- multicultural books
- fantasy
- folktales
- fables
- myths
- historical fiction
- biographies and autobiographies
- poetry
- songbooks
- student-authored books

(Eliason and Jenkins 2003)

nonprofit organizations are also listed. Did you know many organizations across the globe are supporting and promoting the need to bring children closer to nature? What encouraging news!

The resources encourage nature learning while teaching other valuable abstract and concrete concepts and ideas. In addition to connecting them to the curriculum, use the materials to stimulate student interests and senses and creatively cement their understanding of the natural world. Inform families of the resources and how they can access them. As you review the resources, keep a few points in mind:

- Although the continual use of literature and material about nature fosters an "appreciation, understanding, and respect for living things" (Zeece 1999, 161), it must be modeled before children as well.

- Make sure the content of *informational* books for children is current and factual, so that "the world and its inhabitants are portrayed true to nature" (Zeece 1999, 161).

- Literature and other resources should be age- and developmental-level appropriate and connected to children's individual interests. Materials should contain illustrations that captivate and spark children's interest. (Hachey and Butler 2009).

- Book and video selections for children should always be previewed.

The possibilities available to support bringing out a child's nature lover are vast. I hope you find the recommendations useful.

Chapter 1 Resources

Chapter 1 highlights the use of nature to develop a child's sensory awareness, social, literacy, and language skills. It also outlines a variety of gardening projects. Listed are several additional resources to complement the goals described in chapter 1.

RESOURCES TO NURTURE A CHILD'S SENSORY AWARENESS

- Ability Path (www.abilitypath.org)

- Education in Dance and the Related Arts (www .educationindance.org)

- My Special Needs Network (www.myspecialneedsnetwork .com)

- National Network for Child Care (www.nncc.org)

- *Rapunzel's Supermarket: All about Young Children and Their Art* by Ursula Kolbe

SOCIAL, LITERACY, AND LANGUAGE SKILLS RESOURCES

- *Incredible Edible Science: Recipes for Developing Science and Literacy Skills* by Liz Plaster and Rick Krustchinsky

- *The Kid's Guide to Social Action: How to Solve the Social Problems You Choose—and Turn Creative Thinking into Positive Action* by Barbara A. Lewis

- "Playing in the Gutters: Enhancing Children's Cognitive and Social Play" by Sue Dinwiddie. Found at www.community playthings.com/resources/articles/sandandwater/Play Gutters.html.

CHILDREN'S GARDENING RESOURCES

- *A Child's Garden: Sixty Ideas to Make Any Garden Come Alive* by Molly Dannenmaier

- *Easy Garden Projects to Make, Build, and Grow*, edited by Barbara Pleasant and the editors of *Yankee Magazine*

- *Gardening with Children: Brooklyn Botanic Garden All-Region Guide* by Monica Hanneman, Patricia Hulse, Brian Johnson, and Barbara Kurland

- *Handbook of Poisonous and Injurious Plants* by Lewis S. Nelson, Richard D. Shih, Michael Balick, and Andrew Wei

- *Hollyhocks and Honeybees: Garden Projects for Young Children* by Sarah Starbuck, Marla Olthof, and Karen Midden

Nature Spark

Robin Moore's book *Plants for Play* is a great resource for early child care educators and providers to make informed decisions about which plants to use for outdoor play. The book is broken down into sections of sensory variety, play value, seasonal interest, shade quality, screen possibilities, wildlife enhancement, erosion control, and drought tolerance (McGinnis 2002).

- *I Love Dirt! Fifty-Two Activities to Help You and Your Kids Discover the Wonders of Nature* by Jennifer Ward

- *Plants for Play* by Robin C. Moore

· ·

Chapter 2 Resources

Chapter 2 discusses methods for making a classroom more attuned to nature, as well as ideas for incorporating easy, hands-on experiments and learning centers to spark nature connections across the classroom curriculum. Outdoor field trips, hikes, and obstacle courses are also key components of chapter 2. Additional resources follow.

RESOURCES TO ORIENT A CLASSROOM TO NATURE

- "Developing an Outdoor Classroom: Blending Classroom Curriculum and Outdoor Play Space," by M. L. Studer in *Texas Child Care* 2 (1): 12–19 (1998)

- "Outdoor Classroom Adventures" by K. J. Maher in *Science and Children* 37 (5): 20–23 (2000)

- *Outdoor Play, Teaching Strategies with Young Children* by J. P. Perry

RESOURCES FOR EXPERIMENTS AND LEARNING CENTERS

- "Planting the Seeds of Science: The School Garden—a Perfect Laboratory for Teaching Science" by P. Mohrmann in *Instructor* 108 (6): 25–29 (1999)

- *Snails, Trails, and Tadpole Tails: Nature Education for Young Children* by Richard Cohen, Betty Phillips Tunick, and Kurt Seaberg

RESOURCES FOR FIELD TRIPS, HIKES, AND OUTDOOR PLAY

- *The Listening Walk* by Paul Showers and Aliki

- *Ten-Minute Field Trips* by H. R. Russell

Chapter 3 Resources

Chapter 3 discusses the power and importance of play in the natural world to bring out a child's inner nature lover. Using natural elements to create hearty nature-oriented play was also discussed. Examples of play places, special spaces, seats, and stages for children to learn, explore, socialize, and nurture their inner nature lover were presented. The following are additional resources for chapter 3 objectives.

RESOURCES DISCUSSING THE IMPORTANCE OF PLAY

- *Discovering Nature with Young Children* by Ingrid Chalufour and Karen Worth

- *The Ecology of Imagination in Childhood* by Edith Cobb

- *How Children Learn through Play* by Dorothy Einon

- *Last Child in the Woods: Saving Our Children from Nature-Deficit Disorder* by Richard Louv

- *To Play or Not to Play: Is It Really a Question?* by Christine Jeandheur Ferguson and Ernest Dettore Jr.

- *The Power of Play: Learning What Comes Naturally* by David Elkind

- *Sharing Nature with Children* by Joseph Cornell

- *Small Wonders: Nature Education for Young Children* by Linda Garrett, Hannah Thomas, and Hilary Elmer

RESOURCES DISCUSSING NATURAL ELEMENTS TO CREATE HEARTY OUTDOOR PLAY

- *Discovering Nature with Young Children* by Ingrid Chalufour and Karen Worth

- *Exploring Water with Young Children* by Ingrid Chalufour and Karen Worth

- *Play Using Natural Materials* by Alison Howe

- "Playing in the Sand—Naturally" by Ron King, M. Arch, CPSI President, the Natural Playgrounds Company at www .communityplaythings.com/resources/articles /sandandwater/PlaySand.html

- *The Waterhole* by Graeme Base

RESOURCES TO CREATE NATURE-DRIVEN PLAY PLACES, SPECIAL SPACES, SEATS, AND STAGES

- *Children's Special Places: Exploring the Role of Forts, Dens, and Bush Houses in Middle Childhood* by David Sobel

- *Kids' Easy-to-Create Wildlife Habitats: For Small Spaces in City-Suburbs-Countryside* by Emily Stetson

- *Learning with Nature Idea Book: Creating Nurturing Outdoor Spaces for Children* by the National Arbor Day Foundation

- *Natural Playscapes: Creating Outdoor Play Environments for the Soul* by Rusty Keeler

- *Pet Bugs: A Kids' Guide to Catching and Keeping Touchable Insects* by Sally Kneidel

- "Students Are Turning an Empty Lot into an Outdoor Learning Center" by M. Kruglik in *Curriculum Review* 33 (4): 8 (1993)

Chapter 4 Resources

Chapter 4 presents a variety of nature activities to nurture and enhance a child's inner nature lover. Nature-oriented songs, rhymes, and riddles for children to develop abstract and concrete classroom concepts are suggested, and examples of creative, nature-driven sensory materials are explored. The following are more chapter 4 resources.

NATURE CRAFT AND ACTIVITY RESOURCES

- *Discovering Nature with Young Children* by Ingrid Chalufour and Karen Worth

- *Get Out! 150 Easy Ways for Kids and Grown-Ups to Get into Nature and Build a Greener Future* by Judy Molland

- *Organic Crafts: Seventy-Five Earth-Friendly Art Activities* by Kimberly Monaghan

- *Simple Weather Experiments with Everyday Materials* by Muriel Mandel and Frances Zweifel

- *Talking to Fireflies, Shrinking the Moon: Nature Activities for All Ages* by Edward Duensing

RESOURCES FOR NATURE-DRIVEN MUSIC, RHYMES, AND RIDDLES

- *The Bilingual Book of Rhymes, Songs, Stories, and Fingerplays* by Pam Schiller, Rafael Lara-Alecio, and Beverly J. Irby

- *The Complete Book and CD Set of Rhymes, Songs, Poems, Fingerplays, and Chants* by Jackie Silberg and Pam Schiller

- *Jump Rope Rhymes: A Dictionary* by R. Abrahams

- *The Music Box* by Elizabeth Lund Zahniser (www.elzpublishing.com)

- *Nature Notes for Little Folks: Delightfully Entertaining Songs to Celebrate the Outdoors*, CD by Maureen Conlin

- *Oo-pples and Boo-noo-noos: Songs and Activities for Phonemic Awareness* by H. K. Yopp and R. H. Yopp

- Nature sound CDs: visit www.anwo.com

RESOURCES FOR NATURE-DRIVEN SENSORY MATERIALS

- *Beautiful Stuff! Learning with Found Materials* by Cathy Weisman Topal and Lella Gandini

- *Everyday Early Learning: Easy and Fun Activities and Toys Made from Stuff You Can Find around the House* by Jeff A. Johnson with Zoe Johnson

- *The Little Book of Messy Play* by Sally Featherstone and Liz Persse

- *Make Your Own Playdough, Paint, and Other Craft Materials: Easy Recipes to Use with Young Children* by Patricia Caskey

- *Play and Playthings: A Reference Guide* by Bernard Mergen

· ·

Other Great Nature Resources

The following resources will encourage and enhance a nature-driven classroom and curriculum. The books focus on nature involvement, animals, ways to nurture a blooming naturalist, multicultural nature stories, and much more! They will complement all the chapters in *Nature Sparks*.

CHILDREN'S BOOKS FOCUSING ON NATURE INVOLVEMENT

- *Backyard Safaris: Fifty-Two Year-Round Science Adventures* by Phyllis Busch

- *How to Be a Nature Detective* by Millicent Ellis Selsam

- *Nature Watch* by Mick Manning and Britta Granstrom

- *The Pond Book* by Karen Dawe

- *Puddles* by Jonathan London

CHILDREN'S BOOKS WITH "ANIMAL ANTICS"— WONDERFUL INTERACTIVE READ-ALOUDS!

- *Antarctic Antics: A Book of Penguin Poems* by Judy Sierra

- *Big Dog and Little Dog* by Dav Pilkey

- *Chameleons Are Cool* by Martin Jenkins

- *Funny Faces: Monkeys and Apes* by Valerie Tracqui

- *Moo-Ha!* by Bernard Most

CHILDREN'S NATURE BOOKS FOR "TOUCHING AND TEACHING"

- *Baboon* by Kate Banks

- *Baby Animals: Black and White* by Phyllis Limbacher

- *Goodbye-Bye, Daddy!* by Brigitte Weninger

- *One of Each* by Mary Ann Hoberman

FACT AND FICTION BOOKS FOR THE BLOOMING NATURALIST

- *Can We Save Them?* by David Dobson

- *The Jane Goodall Chimpanzee Family Book* by Jane Goodall

- *Mice Squeak, We Speak. A Poem* by Arnold L. Shapiro with illustrations by Tomie dePaola

- *The Tabitha Stories* by A. N. Wilson

MULTICULTURAL NATURE STORIES

- *Brother Eagle, Sister Sky* by Susan Jeffers

- *Creation* by Gerald McDermont

Nature Spark

Read-aloud books are foundational for literacy learning. They are springboards for other creative reading, music, and art activities. Side by Side is an irresistible series of books from Scholastic that invites children to read along. The set of books is designed for collaborative reading and includes *Miss Moo Goes to the Zoo*, *Ladybug's Birthday*, and *Little Raccoon Catches a Cold*. Children will enjoy the rich language and illustrations. Be sure to read books aloud with children one-on-one, not only as a group.

- *Gathering the Sun: An Alphabet in Spanish and English* by Alma Flor Ada

- *One Child, One Seed: A South African Counting Book* by Kathryn Cave and Gisele Wulfsohn

- *Thunder Cake* by Patricia Polacco

CHILDREN'S NATURE MAGAZINES—PERFECT FOR OUTDOOR BOOK NOOKS!

- *National Geographic Young Explorer*

- *Ranger Rick*

- *Ranger Rick's Just for Fun*

- *Wild Animal Baby*

- *Your Big Backyard*

- *Zoobooks*

CHILDREN'S NATURE-ORIENTED CDS AND DVDS

- *Amazing Animals Activity Center* CD-ROM by DK Multimedia

- *Amazing Planet* DVD by National Geographic

- *Creepy Creatures* DVD by National Geographic

- *The Magic School Bus Explores the World of Animals* CD-ROM by Scholastic

- *Swinging Safari* DVD by National Geographic

- *Totally Tropical Rainforest* DVD by National Geographic

- *Wild Animal Adventure* DVD by Baby Einstein

EDUCATIONAL NATURE VIDEOS AND TELEVISION SHOWS

- Disney's *Earth*

- *March of the Penguins*

- Nature programs on PBS, TLC, or the Discovery Channel

- *Sid the Science Kid*

CHILDREN'S NATURE KITS

- Children's Wildlife Kits by Wildforms: Gardening for Wildlife (www.wildforms.co.uk)

Nature Spark

Include resources to support class recycling projects. A fun children's book to add to a classroom library includes, *I Can Save the Earth: One Little Monster Learns to Reduce, Reuse, and Recycle* by Alison Inches. Max, a furry green monster, is cute, but he continually leaves the lights on, never turns his computer off, blasts his television, and constantly clogs the toilet. Max is an environmental nightmare. As a class project, determine materials that can be recycled or reused and how you can conserve water and energy as a class (Crawford et al. 2009).

Nature Spark

There are many well-known national organizations to plug children into for nature-oriented learning and adventure. Consider the following: Audubon Society, Boy Scouts of America, Girl Scouts of America, Natural History Museums, National Forest Service, National Park Service, and National Wildlife Federation

- Getting Started Kit from KaBOOM!

- Junior Forest Ranger Kit, Smokey Bear Headquarters, Washington, DC

- National Geographic offers an assortment of multimedia kits (www.nationalgeographic.com):

  - *The Sun, the Moon*

  - *A Tree through the Seasons*

  - *What Happens in Autumn?*

  - *What Happens in Spring?*

  - *What Happens in Summer?*

  - *What Happens in Winter?*

  - *Why Does It Rain?*

- Scavenger Hunt Kit (www.scavengerhuntsforkids.com)

- Sea and Sage Audubon Society Nature Kits for Loan (www.seaandsageaudubon.org)

- The Young Naturalist's Backpack Kit by Home Science Tools

NATURE-BASED ORGANIZATIONS AND CLUBS

- EarthPlay Network (www.earthplay.net)

- Evergreen (www.evergreen.ca)

- Imagineaction (www.imagine-action.ca)

- Jane Goodall's Roots and Shoots (www.janegoodall.org)

- KaBOOM! (www.kaboom.org)

- National Wildlife Federation (www.nwf.org)

NATURAL PLAY AND TEACHING WEBSITES

- Growing a Green Generation—http://extension.unh.edu/news/2006/03/growing_a_green_generation_chi.html

- Growing Minds, Farm to School—www.growing-minds.org

- Junior Master Gardener—www.jmgkids.us

- My First Garden—www.urbanext.illinois.edu/firstgarden

WEATHER REPORTING AND RESEARCHING RESOURCES

- *Can It Really Rain Frogs?* by Spencer Christian

- *Feel the Wind* by Arthur Dorros

- *Hurricanes* by Arlene Erlbach

- *Lightning* by Stephen Karma

- *Snow Is Falling* by Franklyn Branley

- *Tornadoes Can Make It Rain Crabs* by Melvin Berger

- The Weather Channel Kids (www.theweatherchannel
  kids.com)

- *What Will the Weather Be?* by Linda DeWitt

NATURE BOOKS ABOUT SORTING, CLASSIFYING, COMPARING, AND ADDING

- *Bunches and Bunches of Bunnies* by Louise Mathews

- *How Many Snails? A Counting Book* by Paul Giganti Jr.

- *Rooster's Off to See the World* by Eric Carle

NATURE-AWARENESS PICTURE BOOKS FOR TEACHERS OF CHILDREN AGES THREE TO NINE

- *The Dandelion Seed* by Joseph P. Anthony

- *A Drop around the World* by Barbara Shaw McKinney

- *Play Lightly on the Earth* by Jacqueline Horsfall

- *Walking with Mama* by Barbara Stynes

- *Wonderful Nature, Wonderful You* by Karin Ireland

Nature Spark

"Fold Out and Find Out" nature books are irresistible to children. Listed here are two must-haves for your classroom library!

- *Little Green Frogs*
- *YUCK*

Closing Thoughts

According to Richard Louv, author of *Last Child in the Woods: Saving Our Children from Nature-Deficit Disorder* (2005), a growing body of evidence indicates that contact with nature is as important to children as good nutrition and adequate sleep, and therefore educators need to address children's access to nature. A nature-based curriculum does indeed support a child's development and learning in academic, social, and health-related domains. The focus of any play activity for children, whether they are indoors or out, should remain on the process as it unfolds, not the end product that is produced. Bringing out a child's inner nature lover can be accomplished in today's media-driven society, even in the most urban of environments and the smallest of spaces. Don't forget your end goal—equipping students to understand, connect with, and observe the power and beauty of nature in an ever-changing world. Stay focused on planting nature seeds of wonderment and a thirst for the outdoors using the activities, lessons, and resources presented in this book—then leave the rest up to Mother Nature.

References

Aquascape, Inc. 2011. *Ponds for Kids Activities Guide*. www.aquascapeinc
.com/contractors/ponds_for_kids.

Arnosky, Jim. 2002. *Field Trips: Bug Hunting, Animal Tracking, Bird-
Watching, and Shore Watching*. New York: HarperCollins.

Bellanca, James, Carolyn Chapman, and Elizabeth Swartz. 1997.
Multiple Assessments for Multiple Intelligences. 3rd ed. Arlington
Heights, IL: IRI/Skylight Training and Publishing Inc.

Benson, Jennifer, and Jennifer Leeper Miller. 2008. "Experiences in
Nature: A Pathway to Standards." *Young Children* 63 (4): 22–28.

Carson, Rachel. 1956. *The Sense of Wonder*. New York: HarperCollins.

Chalufour, Ingrid, and Karen Worth. 2003. *Discovering Nature with
Young Children*. St. Paul, MN: Redleaf Press.

Copple, Carol, and Sue Bredekamp. 2008. "Getting Clear about
Developmentally Appropriate Practice." *Young Children* 63 (1): 54–55.

———, eds. 2009. *Developmentally Appropriate Practice in Early
Childhood Programs Serving Children from Birth through Age 8*, 3rd ed.
Washington, DC: National Association for the Education of Young
Children.

Cornett, Claudia E. 2003. *Creating Meaning through Literature and the
Arts: An Integrated Resource for Classroom Teachers*. Upper Saddle
River, NJ: Prentice Hall.

Crawford, Elizabeth Outlaw, Emily T. Heaton, Karen Heslop, and
Kassandra Kixmiller. 2009. "Science Learning at Home: Involving
Families." *Young Children* 64 (6): 39–41.

Curtis, Deb, and Margie Carter. 2005. "Rethinking Early Childhood
Environments to Enhance Learning." *Young Children* 60 (3): 34–38.

Danoff-Burg, James A. 2002. "Be a Bee and Other Approaches to
Introducing Young Children to Entomology." *Young Children* 57 (5):
42–47.

Drew, Walter F., and Baji Rankin. 2004. "Promoting Creativity for
Life Using Open-Ended Materials." *Young Children* 59 (4): 38–45.

Eliason, Claudia, and Loa Jenkins. 2003. *A Practical Guide to Early
Childhood Curriculum*. 7th ed. Upper Saddle River, NJ: Merrill
Prentice Hall.

Giles, Martha Mead. 1991. "A Little Background Music, Please."
Principal 71 (2): 41–44.

Ginsburg, Kenneth R., and Martha M. Jablow. 2006. *A Parent's Guide to Building Resilience in Children and Teens: Giving Your Child Roots and Wings*. Elk Grove Village, IL: American Academy of Pediatrics.

Griffin, Christina, and Brad Rinn. 1998. "Enhancing Outdoor Play with an Obstacle Course." *Young Children* 53 (3): 18–26.

Hachey, Alyse C., and Deanna L. Butler. 2009. "Seeds in the Window, Soil in the Sensory Table: Science Education through Gardening and Nature-Based Play." *Young Children* 64 (6): 42–48.

Hammerman, Donald R., William M. Hammerman, and Elizabeth L. Hammerman. 2001. *Teaching in the Outdoors*. 5th ed. Danville, IL: Interstate Publishers, Inc.

Harris, Elizabeth. 2008. *Yikes! Wow! Yuck! Fun Experiments for Your First Science Fair*. New York: Lark Books.

Hauser, Jill. 1998. *Science Play: Beginning Discoveries for Two- to Six-Year-Olds*. Charlotte, VT: Williamson Publishing.

Henderson, Tara Zollinger, and David J. Atencio. 2007. "Integration of Play, Learning, and Experience: What Museums Afford Young Visitors." *Early Childhood Education Journal* 35 (3): 245–51.

Hill-Clarke, Kantaylieniere Y., and Nicole R. Robinson. 2004. "It's as Easy as A-B-C and Do-Re-Mi: Music, Rhythm, and Rhyme Enhance Children's Literacy Skills." *Young Children* 59 (5): 91–95.

Hirschfeld, Robert, and Nancy White. 1995. *The Kids' Science Book: Creative Experiences for Hands-On Fun*. Charlotte, VT: Williamson Publishing.

Honig, Alice Sterling. 2004. "Exploring Nature with Babies." *Early Childhood Today* 18 (6): 22.

———. 2007. "Play: Ten Power Boosts for Children's Early Learning." *Young Children* 62 (5): 72–78.

Humphryes, Janet. 2000. "Exploring Nature with Children." *Young Children* 55 (2): 16–20.

Isaacs, Susan. 1929. *The Nursery Years: The Mind of the Child from Birth to Six Years*. London: Routledge.

———. 1946. *Social Development in Young Children: A Study of Beginnings*. London: Routledge.

Jones, Nancy P. 2005. "Big Jobs: Planning for Competence." *Young Children* 60 (2): 86–93.

Johnson, June. 1997. *838 Ways to Amuse a Child*. New York: Gramercy Books.

Kalmar, Kathy. 2008. "Let's Give Children Something to Talk About: Oral Language and Preschool Literacy." *Young Children* 63 (1): 88–92.

Keeler, Rusty. 2008. *Natural Playscapes: Creating Outdoor Play Environments for the Soul*. Redmond, WA: Exchange Press.

Korte, Katrina M., Laura Jane Fielden, and Josephine Agnew. 2005. "To Run, Stomp, or Study: Hissing Cockroaches in the Classroom." *Young Children* 60 (2): 12–18.

Kostelnik, Marjorie J. 1993. "Recognizing the Essentials of Developmentally Appropriate Practice." *Exchange* (March/April): 73–77.

Kostelnik, Marjorie J., Anne K. Soderman, and Alice P. Whiren. 2004. *Developmentally Appropriate Curriculum: Best Practice in Early Childhood Education*. 3rd ed. Upper Saddle River, NJ: Prentice Hall.

Louv, Richard. 2005. *Last Child in the Woods: Saving Our Children from Nature-Deficit Disorder*. New York: Workman Publishing.

McGinnis, Janet. 2002. "Enriching the Outdoor Environment." *Young Children* 57 (3): 28–30.

Miles, Lisa Rounds. 2009. "The General Store: Reflections on Children at Play." *Young Children* 64 (4): 36–41.

Moomaw, Sally, and Brenda Hieronymus. 1997. *More Than Magnets: Exploring the Wonders of Science in Preschool and Kindergarten*. St. Paul, MN: Redleaf Press.

Moore, R. C. 1980. "Generating Relevant Urban Childhood Places: Learning from the 'Yard.'" In *Play in Human Settlements*, edited by P. F. Wilkonson, 45–75. London: Croom Helm.

Muir, John. 1911. *My First Summer in the Sierra*. Boston: Houghton Mifflin.

Myhre, Susan M. 1993. "Enhancing Your Dramatic-Play Area through the Use of Prop Boxes." *Young Children* 48 (5): 6–13.

National Environmental Education Foundation. 2011. "Fact Sheet: Children's Health and Nature." Health and Environment Program: Children and Nature Initiative. www.neefusa.org/assets/files /NIFactSheet.pdf.

Odoy, Hilary Ann Donato, and Sarah Hanna Foster. 1997. "Creating Play Crates for the Outdoor Classroom." *Young Children* 52 (6): 12–16.

Pica, Rae. 2009. "Can Movement Promote Creativity?" *Young Children* 64 (4): 60–61.

Rettig, Michael. 2005. "Using the Multiple Intelligences to Enhance Instruction for Young Children and Young Children with Disabilities." *Early Childhood Education Journal* 32 (4): 255–59.

Rogers, Liz, and Dana Steffan. 2009. "Clay Play." *Young Children* 60 (1): 22–27.

Rosenow, Nancy. 2008. "Learning to Love the Earth . . . and Each Other." *Young Children* 63 (1): 10–14.

Ross, Michael E. 2000. "Science Their Way." *Young Children* 55 (2): 6–13.

Russo, Michele, Susan Gallagher Colurciello, and Rebecca Kelly. 2008. "For the Birds! Seeing, Being, and Creating the Bird World." *Young Children* 61 (1): 26–30.

Satterlee, Donna, and Grace D. Cormons. 2008. "Sparking Interest in Nature." *Young Children* 63 (1): 16–20.

Shore, Rebecca, and Janis Strasser. 2006. "Music for Their Minds." *Young Children* 61 (2): 62–67.

Silberg, Jackie. 2004. *The Learning Power of Laughter: Over 300 Playful Activities and Ideas That Promote Learning with Young Children.* Beltsville, MD: Gryphon House.

Snyder, Susan. 1997. "Developing Musical Intelligence: Why and How." *Early Childhood Education Journal* 24 (3): 165–71.

Sobel, David. 1993. *Children's Special Places.* Tucson, AZ: Zephyr Press.

———. 1996. *Beyond Ecophobia: Reclaiming the Heart in Nature Education.* Great Barrington, MA: The Orion Society and The Myrin Institute.

Starbuck, Sara, and Marla Olthof. 2008. "Involving Families and Community through Gardening." *Young Children* 63 (5): 74–79.

Sutterby, John A., and Joe L. Frost. 2002. "Making Playgrounds Fit for Children and Children Fit on Playgrounds." *Young Children* 57 (3): 36–41.

Talbot, James, and Joe L. Frost. 1989. "Magical Playscapes." *Childhood Education* 66:11–19.

Tee, Ong Puay. 2004. "Innovative Use of Local Resources for Children's Play: A Case in Malaysia." *Young Children* 59 (5): 14–18.

Thompson, Sharon. 1994. "What's a Clothesline Doing on the Playground?" *Young Children* 50 (1): 70–71.

Torquati, Julia, and Jana Barber. 2005. "Dancing with Trees: Infants and Toddlers in the Garden." *Young Children* 60 (3): 40–46.

Tu, Tsunghui. 2006. "Preschool Science Environment: What Is Available in a Preschool Classroom?" *Early Childhood Education Journal* 33 (4): 245–51.

Watson, Amy, and Rebecca McCathren. 2009. "Including Children with Special Needs: Are You and Your Early Childhood Program Ready?" *Young Children* 64 (2): 20–26.

White, Jan. 2008. *Playing and Learning Outdoors: Making Provision for High-Quality Experiences in the Outdoor Environment.* New York: Routledge.

Wilson, Ruth. 1997. "A Sense of Place." *Early Childhood Education Journal* 24 (3): 191–94.

Woyke, Priscilla P. 2004. "Hopping Frogs and Trail Walks: Connecting Young Children and Nature." *Young Children* 59 (1): 82–85.

Yopp, Hallie Kay, and Ruth Helen Yopp. 2009. "Phonological Awareness Is Child's Play." *Young Children* 64 (1): 12–21.

Zeece, Pauline Davey. 1999. "Things of Nature and the Nature of Things: Natural Science-Based Literature for Young Children." *Early Childhood Education Journal* 26 (3): 161–66.

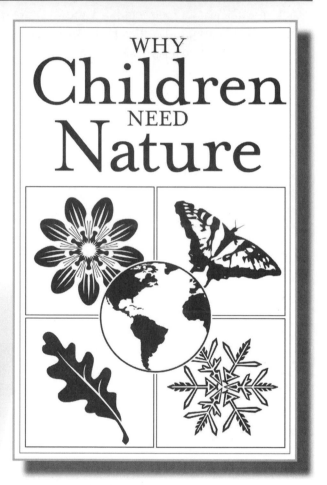